TOM GROSSMAN SR.

Author of *The Praying Church*

Also by the author:

The Praying Church

For more information contact:

praychurchpray.com

214-680-6478

TABLE OF CONTENTS

1

THE GREAT TRAP

To have a great trap the bait must be irresistible-

A few years from today...

You wake up on Saturday with no access to the internet. What happened? You just spent last night at home, celebrating with friends what seemed to be the greatest event in human history. For the first time, a man had been appointed as Lord of all the Earth. This man was thought for many months to be the Messiah of Israel. But now, it seems that the whole world believes that he is really God on Earth.

Amazing! But does it really matter right now?

Because at this moment you have bigger fish to fry. You can't get on the internet, and that's the real problem. Without access to the internet you can't read the news, pay for bills, buy groceries, or get to your savings or retirement account. Of course, the real tragedy is that you can't watch Netflix!

You try every which way, but nothing will get you online. You try to call the bank, but your smartphone is also locked. You know you paid your bill. You decide to drive to the bank, but you are locked out of your new high-tech car. Now, for the first time in years neighbors are milling together outside.

Okay, it's not just you. This is a bigger difficulty than you thought. As you walk toward them, they are talking about everything from a major cyberattack to an overload of the internet being caused by all the people pledging loyalty to the new world leader appointed just last night.

So, you decide to walk the half mile to the 7-Eleven to use their phone and buy some supplies. One of the neighbors shouts out, "You better take some cash." When you get there, you realize your neighbor was right. There is a line of people shouting at the cashier because their cash cards won't work.

The day goes by and your family and neighbors, for the first time, feel the pain of not being connected to the outside world. Smartphones, big screens and our high-tech cars are all connected to the internet. To make matters worse, your electricity goes off. There's no storm or heat wave, it just goes off. Rumors swirl through your darkened neighborhood, and one thing is certain—you and your neighbors are stuck.

The following morning you check to see if there has been any change. As you open your computer notebook there is an alert on the screen. What a relief!

Here's what it says:

CITIZENS: By now you know that the global internet system had been brought to a stop. A group of extremists took credit for this act of terror. This happened within hours of our new leader taking his place in the Jerusalem temple and receiving the joyous support from the leaders of every nation.

Our Lord quickly gathered the best of the best, and after working around the clock, the internet crisis is now over, and the terrorists have been captured. This quick work has restored world order and internet service is again available to all. However, the shutdown was so devasting that global leaders voted unanimously to put internet control under the oversight of our new leader and Messiah.

It is vital to the security of the world that the internet, as well as your connection, stays safe and secure. For your protection, our Messiah insists that only those who pledge their personal allegiance and devotion to his leadership and the new world order will be allowed to use this important service to mankind.

WARNING: This pledge should not be taken lightly. It, in fact, signifies that you belong to this new world order and pledge your heart and soul to its success. This vow signifies a new covenant between all who receive this emblem of solidarity and our leader. The Messiah promises to protect you and provide for you during his reign; in turn, you promise loyalty to him.

It's easy. A new app has been downloaded to every internet device. Those who pledge their allegiance will place their right palm or index finger on the square box appearing on their smartphone or computer screen. When it reads your print, it will light up. You will then look closely into the same box and your iris will be scanned. When you hear a three-second beep, your system will be open. You will use this simple biometric process one time and your systems will run smoothly and securely. All of your banking and other benefits will be instantly restored.

4

However, If the system *ever* detects an intruder, it will lock. Only those who pledge dedication to our Lord and Messiah will be allowed access to the internet from this point forward.

With one brilliant move on the global chessboard, this new leader, backed by a delegation of prime ministers and kings, has taken control.

This man of peace has been charming the nations for the past several years. Now everything is changing. He has stepped into his role as the long-awaited Antichrist, also known as the Beast of the book of Revelation.

Now, not only will those who refuse allegiance to this false Christ be shut out of the internet, they will also be hunted down and put to death.

Why? Those who pledge allegiance to the beast will be possessed with powerful demonic energy. They will have no conscience and their hearts will be consumed with rage against those who resist their master.

This act by the beast, will fulfill a host of Bible prophecies that we will examine in this book. We will discover why these prophecies have been mostly hidden from the modern American church and why, only now, can they be fulfilled.

5

Revelation 13:15b-17 *All who refused to worship the image [of the beast are] to be killed. ¹⁶ It [he]also forced all people, great and small, rich and poor, free and slave, to receive a mark on their right hands or on their foreheads, ¹⁷ so that they could not buy or sell unless they had the mark, which is the name of the beast or the number of its name.*

In this book we will take a deep dive into the prophecy taught by Jesus and the Apostles, Paul and John. Read in their words the clear warning of a false global messiah and a worldwide trap.

Warning: This subject is not for the faint of heart.

2

How Did We Get Here?

2 Thessalonians 2:1-2a *Concerning the coming of our Lord Jesus Christ and our being gathered to him, we ask you, brothers and sisters, ² not to become easily unsettled or alarmed by the teaching allegedly from us—whether by a prophecy or by word of mouth or by letter—*

This is a solemn warning by the apostle Paul. It was written to the church he had recently started. This church was misinterpreting what he taught them regarding the return of Jesus Christ.

Is it possible that subsequent generations, including our own, have done the same thing?

We only need to look at the people's expectations during the time of Christ in the first century AD. Before Christ's miraculous birth, there had been prophesies going back more than a thousand years which spoke of a time when God would send a Messiah to deliver His people and reign on the Earth victoriously.

Israel's Initial Expectation

The Pharisees, religious leaders, scholars, teachers, and ordinary Jewish people of Jesus' day were looking for this Messiah. It had been prophesied that a leader like King David of old would come on the scene, conquer their enemies, and rule over Israel. This was the Messiah they wanted.

Here are two examples:

Psalm 2:7-12 *I will proclaim the LORD's decree: He said to me, "You are my son; today I have become your father. 8 Ask me, and I will make the nations your inheritance, the ends of the Earth your possession. 9 You will break them with a rod of iron; you will dash them to pieces like pottery." 10 Therefore, you kings, be wise; be warned, you rulers of the Earth. 11 Serve the LORD with fear and celebrate his rule with trembling. 12 Kiss his son, or he will be angry, and your way will lead to your destruction, for his wrath can flare up in a moment. Blessed are all who take refuge in him.*

Daniel 7:13-14 *In my vision at night I looked, and there before me was one like a son of man, coming with the clouds of heaven. He approached the Ancient of Days and was led into his presence. ¹⁴ He was given authority, glory and sovereign power; all nations and peoples of every language worshiped him. His dominion is an everlasting dominion that will not pass away, and his kingdom is one that will never be destroyed.*

There are numerous passages like these, and faithful Jewish people would have heard and trusted in them since their youth. Again, their expectation was to have a powerful messiah that would rule the nations; a messiah before whom kings would bow down.

Jesus' First Coming

The New Testament gives explicit details about the Messiah's coming. But instead of the powerful Messiah they hoped for, they received a humble servant who died shamefully on a cross. The cross was God's plan for Christ's first coming. In addition, Jesus's death on the cross fulfilled many prophecies. Let us look at an important example from 750 years before Jesus was born.

Isaiah 53:4-6 *Surely, he [Jesus] took up our pain and bore our suffering, yet we considered him punished by God, stricken by him, and afflicted.* *5 But he was pierced for our transgressions, he was crushed for our iniquities; the punishment that brought us peace was on him, and by his wounds we are healed. 6 We all, like sheep, have gone astray, each of us has turned to our own way; and the LORD has laid on him the iniquity of us all.*

When we look at this passage or others like it, we know that this is obviously referring to Jesus Christ, God's Messiah, or the anointed One. Additionally, we know that He was a human descendant of King David. Even though He was flesh and blood like all men, He also had a powerful, supernatural aspect to His life. He was born of a virgin, fully God and fully man without sin.

The common people recognized this about Jesus and called Him the "Son of David". This is a term reserved for the flawless and supernatural calling to sit on David's eternal throne. The term "Son" alluded to His divinity. (Psalm 132:11, Jeremiah 33:17)

Matthew 9:27 *As Jesus went on from there, two blind men followed him, calling out, "Have mercy on us, **Son of David**!"*

Matthew 12:23 *All the people were astonished and said, "Could this be the* **Son of David***?"*

Matthew 21:15 *But when the chief priests and the teachers of the law saw the wonderful things he did and the children shouting in the temple courts, "Hosanna to the* **Son of David***," they were indignant.*

John 6:15 *Jesus, knowing that they intended to come and make him* **king** *by force, withdrew again to a mountain by himself.*

Many of the Jewish people, and especially their religious leaders, could not reconcile the fact that these two seemingly opposing pictures of the Messiah were the same person. The conquering King revealed in Psalm 2 and Daniel 7 was what they expected. Yet the suffering Savior from Isaiah 53 was what they got. These leaders and those who were seeking to overthrow Rome were unimpressed with Jesus.

Consequently, the Jewish leaders concluded that Jesus was a false prophet. To them he was a phony Messiah who was born under questionable circumstances, to a purported virgin, and in a stable, no less.

What's more, Jesus displayed no inclination or ambition to advance into the leadership circle of the Pharisees or Sadducees. Instead, He was an outsider like His cousin John the Baptist. In their eyes, He was unpredictable, disruptive, and uninvolved in the nation's politics.

Jesus spent His short 3½ year ministry meeting with sinners, harlots, and the poor. His closest followers were common men, people who were rough around the edges. Jesus taught the crowds about mercy, compassion and love. He healed the diseased and ministered to the demonized. There were rumors that He even raised a few people from the dead.

The Jewish leaders were afraid that Jesus would provoke an uprising against them and the Roman government. Such a scenario would cost them their privileged position in society and undoubtedly provoke a heavy-handed response from the Roman authorities. Their best hope was to find a charge against Him that was worthy of death. You know the story.

The Second Coming Dilemma

It is true that the first coming of the Messiah was hard to accept while Jesus still walked the Earth. How could a suffering Savior and conquering King be the same person? Jesus had a difficult time explaining this dichotomy regarding His first and His second comings to His disciples. How much more difficult this teaching was for the ordinary people.

Jesus' immediate disciples were confused about His real purpose during the entire 3½ years that He walked in the flesh with them. We must bear in mind that the people of Israel were anticipating a conquering King, and that expectation was shared by His twelve apostles as well. Although these people were alive on the Earth alongside Jesus and were eyewitnesses to His mighty ministry, they were confused. Similarly, it shouldn't be surprising that there is confusion regarding His second coming today.

In Luke 9, Jesus told the twelve apostles for the **first time** that He is going to be put to death.

Luke 9:22 *And he said, "The Son of Man must suffer many things and be rejected by the elders, the chief priests and the teachers of the law, and he must be killed and on the third day be raised to life."*

Nine days later a **second warning** came.

Luke 9:44-46 *"Listen carefully to what I am about to tell you: The Son of Man is going to be delivered into the hands of men."* *45 But they* did not understand what this meant. It was hidden from them, so that they did not grasp it, and they were afraid to ask him about it. *⁴⁶ An argument started among the disciples as to which of them would be the greatest.*

Stop and think about this: their leader was telling them that He was going to be killed in a few days, and they could not grasp it. They were afraid to ask Him to explain this. What did they really want? They wanted to know who would be the greatest in His new kingdom. Again, they were perceiving circumstances through their false expectations.

He said the same thing to His disciples a **third time,** "I will be put to death." True to form, it passed over their heads due to an incorrect perspective.

Luke 18:31-33 *Then He took the twelve aside and said to them, "Behold, we are going up to Jerusalem, and all things which are written through the prophets about the Son of Man will be accomplished. ³² For He will be] handed over to the Gentiles, and will be mocked and mistreated and spit upon, ³³ and after they have scourged Him, they will kill Him; and the third day He will rise again."*

How did the disciples respond?

Verse 34 *But the disciples understood **none** of these things, and the meaning of this statement was hidden from them, and they did not comprehend the things that were said.*

They understood **none** of these things. Despite three distinct warnings, their expectations did not shift.

Forty days after Pentecost they still thought Jesus was going to "restore the kingdom" immediately as a conquering Messiah King.

Acts 1:6 *Then they (the disciples) gathered around him and asked him, "Lord, are you at this time going to restore the kingdom to Israel?"*

Acts 1: 7-8 *He said to them: "It is not for you to know the times or dates the Father has set by his own authority. 8 But you will receive power when the Holy Spirit comes on you; and you will be my witnesses in Jerusalem, and in all Judea and Samaria, and to the ends of the Earth."*

They still wanted to see Israel restored as it was in King David's time, the zenith in the nation's history.

Additionally, when Jesus said to them, *"you will be my witnesses…to the ends of the Earth"*, the early believers had no clue how far the "ends of the Earth" were or how long it would take to accomplish the task.

Think about this for a moment: Jesus' own apostles still could not conceive that His first coming was to die for the sins of the world and not to reign as a visible king. How could they ever understand the 2,000-year gap between His first and second comings?

This misunderstanding by His own disciples becomes a stumbling block for believers today. We fall prey to the following logic: "Even Jesus' own disciples thought that He would return in their lifetimes. Why should we expect to be better informed than they were?"

The answer? A few years after Jesus' ascension to heaven, the Apostles began to record Jesus' original words and teachings in what we call the New Testament!

In the next chapter, we will see that Jesus also taught thoroughly about His second coming. It is very straightforward. However, with a 2,000-year gap between Jesus' first and second coming, we observe that this confusion only intensifies.

Time plus cultural and political change equals confusion, doubt, and false expectations.

Certainly, over time believers have come to better understand the purpose of Jesus' first coming. He revealed Himself as the suffering servant, or Lamb of God, who was sent by the Father to take away the sins of the world. We understand that the gospel is the good news and that God is offering peace to sinful, rebellious mankind. The Father is offering a full pardon for sin and an invitation to be adopted into His family. He offers an inheritance with Jesus which makes those who believe wealthier than billionaires.

This gospel is truly great news. Nonetheless, believers over time started asking questions such as the following: "What about the conquering king?" "When do we get to see the Messiah?" Then centuries and millennia passed. "Will He ever come?" or "Maybe we totally misunderstood the prophecies in the first place?" "Were all those promises about a second coming symbolic?" "Could it be that Jesus did all of His conquering in the form by overcoming *sin, death and the grave?*" "Perhaps Jesus has already returned by living in us." "Maybe Jesus will come secretly in the night like a thief, and no one will even know what happened."

Over time we became and are still terribly confused about the second coming of Jesus.

When and where did the confusion start? Obviously, the first apostles and disciples had no idea of the enormity of preaching to the "ends of the Earth". Then they all started to die off, and not due to natural causes but rather to martyrdom.

- Within thirty-five to forty years after the resurrection of Jesus, eleven of the original twelve apostles were dead. Judas hung himself, but all the rest except John were put to death for their testimony about Jesus. They claimed that the suffering servant rose from the dead and was returning as the true Messiah.

- In 70 AD the Jewish temple was destroyed. Many thousands of Jews were slaughtered, and the remainder were scattered to the nations. Not only was there no temple in Jerusalem, the nation of Israel ceased to exist.

- These facts, together with the continued growth of the Roman persecution, began to sow doubt into the believers' minds about how, when, or even if Jesus would return.

- To give fresh hope, around 95 AD God gave the "Revelation of Jesus Christ", which is the final book of the Bible. This was a significant encouragement, nevertheless the passage of time, persecution of the church, and destruction of the Jewish temple reveal that something important was missing from their understanding.

- Since the book of Revelation includes abundant Old Testament symbolism, it has become easy to brush off the return of Christ with the following comments: "It's all symbolic." "It's too confusing." "It will all work out." "In the end we win." It's safe to say that the book of Revelation has always been something of an enigma to the church.

Then a Big Change

- Around 325 AD the Roman Emperor, Constantine, had an open vision of the cross and was converted to Christianity. Next, he did something amazing—**He made Christianity the official religion of the Roman Empire!** For almost three hundred years Christians were persecuted by Rome. Then suddenly, Christianity was exalted. A new form of Christianity was spawned, a religion with the backing and resources of the Roman Empire.

- Over time it became illegal for Roman citizens to not believe in Christ. The Roman government bankrolled cathedrals, convents, schools, hospitals, and paid leadership. Because of the size and scope of the church, training for leaders and liturgical procedures became standardized. Before long, nearly every church met under the banner of the Holy Roman Catholic Church. Essentially, church meetings were standardized, and the system became the only way for people to worship.

- With a government-backed church, the original persecution of Christians was reversed. Now, anyone who opposed the church became an enemy of the state!

- Over time and in spite of great resistance from the Roman church, there were challenges to the Roman Catholic authority and eventual break-offs. This resistance produced the Eastern Orthodox, Lutheran, Anglican, Presbyterian, Baptist, and Methodist churches as well as many smaller, lesser-known groups. Having the right answers about the second coming mattered little because with no Jewish temple or nation of Israel, almost no one believed that Jesus would return any time soon.

- With these changes and the passage of time, the return of the Lord took a back seat to other priorities like developing and interpreting theology, reformation, politics, wars, epidemics, famines, and disasters.

Remember, from 70 AD until 1948 Israel did not exist as a sovereign nation. What's more, the Jewish temple was destroyed and lay under centuries of ruin. Quite simply, the prophecies regarding Jesus' return could not be fulfilled. There will be more about this in subsequent chapters.

Why must we re-examine our beliefs as Christians now?

- Since 1948, Israel has been restored as a nation. and recently the Unites States recognized Jerusalem as its capital. This is an unheard-of miracle where a conquered nation that was erased from the face of the Earth for 1,878 years reappears with its language and customs intact. This phenomenon makes way for the rebuilding of the Jewish temple.

- Significantly, it is the reconstruction of the Jewish Temple that will appear as a Global wonder and simultaneously turn out to be the greatest religious, political, and military trap ever sprung in history.

- The technological explosion with its intricate global networking has made it possible for just about every human with a smartphone, PC, cash card or other devices to be spied on and tracked. The internet, only in existence since 1990, is the vehicle through which we now buy and sell, receive checks, pay our bills and shop.

- There is a sinister side to all of this technology as well, and it will play a huge role before the return of Christ.

- In the very near future, a faithful remnant of the church actually will become what Jesus called His "house of prayer". See Luke 11:17. This movement has been multiplying in seed form for sixty years and will soon explode. As you will see, "the prayers of the saints" will fuel the spread of the gospel and the release of power on the Earth.

- The gospel is being preached to the "ends of the Earth" just as Jesus prophesied in **Matthew 24:14**: *"And this gospel of the kingdom will be preached in the whole world as a testimony to all nations, and then the end will come."*

- Now, almost 2,000 years after the resurrection of Christ and the birth of Christianity, we are living in those days in which the gospel has gone to the ends of the Earth. In the last fifty years it is estimated that **3.9 billion** Bibles have been printed. That comes out to about two Bibles per household. The New Testament has been translated into **1,521 languages** and portions of the Bible into **1,121** other languages.

The job is nearly complete. Fueled by prayer and Holy Spirit-inspired vision, men and women in the mission movement using modern technology will wrap up the work in the next few years.

Today's Christian Expectation

It has been 2,000 years since the Jewish people and their leaders were confused about the first coming of Christ. They expected a conquering King to come and overthrow Rome. Instead they got the suffering servant, the Lamb of God.

What are you expecting? What is your church or denomination expecting? Why is there so much confusion that most pastors avoid the subject of Christs' return altogether?

This is a very dangerous time for the church worldwide. Imagine living in Europe in 1933, just a few years before the world exploded in war and butchery. Over fifty million people died and over six million European Jews were singled out for genocide.

Think what it would have been like to live in Europe through that season of terror as a Jew while your world came under the murderous grip of a diabolical dictator.

We can hope that the world would have learned its lesson from that catastrophe, which occurred just one generation ago. Tragically, this is not the case. Listen to what Jesus says in His end time teaching.

Matthew 24:21 *For then there will be great distress, unequaled from the beginning of the world until now—and never to be equaled again.*

Revelation 1:3

Blessed is the one who reads aloud the words of this prophecy and blessed are those who hear it and take to heart what is written in it, because the time is near.

3

WHAT DID JESUS REALLY TEACH HIS TWELVE DISCIPLES ABOUT HIS RETURN?

Matthew 24:3-5 *As Jesus was sitting on the Mount of Olives, the disciples came to him privately. "Tell us," they said, "when will this happen, and what will be the sign of your coming and of the end of the age?" 4 Jesus answered: "Watch out that no one deceives you. 5 For many will come in my name, claiming, 'I am the Messiah,' and will deceive many."*

Instead of going through all the various end time teachings and attempting to point out their flaws, I am simply going to show you what Jesus taught His twelve apostles. It is important to read these passages in context.

Much of the end time confusion comes from Bible teachers living after 70 AD—and before 1948. We examined this in chapter one. They were trying to discover a way for the return of Jesus to work out without a nation of Israel or a Jewish Temple. Certainly, we are still waiting for the temple to be rebuilt. Yet all that is required is a sliver of time in which the political dynamic allows its reconstruction.

In Israel, elaborate plans and provision are all in place to proceed with the construction of the temple at full speed, as soon as the moment presents itself. At that point, all of the physical prerequisites will be in place for the end time scenario to enable Jesus' return.

As mentioned in chapter one, the problem with false expectations is that they lead to disillusionment. Disillusioned people are simply disappointed. We get let down when things do not work out as expected. We then can become discouraged and depressed.

In small matters of disappointment, often we can recover easily. For instance, if my favorite restaurant runs out of Coke Zero, I can bounce back to normal in about twenty seconds with Diet Pepsi. What happens, though, when one of my young children is killed in a car accident, or I am diagnosed with stage four cancer, or if my wife suddenly passes away without warning? Some people may recover emotionally in a month or two, but others never do.

The point is obvious...

Is it possible that some of the end time scenarios that are being taught in the church are preparing the people of God for a major disappointment? As a believer, you will need to decide if your church is stepping into a snare. If you are unsure, it should become obvious as you read on.

Here is a warning from Jesus about this very issue while speaking of the days preceding His return:

Luke 21:34-36 *"Be careful, or your hearts will be weighed down with carousing, drunkenness and the anxieties of life, and that day will close on you suddenly like a trap. 35 For it will come on all those who live on the face of the whole Earth. 36 Be always on the watch, and pray that you may be able to escape all that is about to happen, and that you may be able to stand before the Son of Man."*

Yes, not only will the lost be trapped, but also those who have lived their lives as believers yet still did not understand and prepare for His return. They become dissipated and loaded down with activity, or they sit numb in front of a TV screen or computer.

Review

Each of the four gospels begins with the first coming of Christ and His earthly ministry. This was discussed in the previous chapter. We know the story of His first coming and celebrate it each Christmas and Easter season.

The first coming was explained in the writings of David in the Psalms and in the writings of the prophets. Up to this current moment in history, the conquering King Jesus has yet to arrive.

Because of the end time confusion that we explored in chapter one, we must take a fresh look at this subject in the Bible. Our task as believers and students of the Bible is not to protect our own ideas nor the ideas that we learned from someone else, but rather truly to become students ourselves. The Apostle Peter cited the Old Testament prophets as examples of this.

1 Peter 1:10-11 *Concerning this salvation, the prophets, who spoke of the grace that was to come to you, searched intently and with the greatest care, 11 trying to find out the time and circumstances to*

29

which the Spirit of Christ in them was pointing when he predicted the sufferings of the Messiah and the glories that would follow.

If the Old Testament prophets were searching diligently into the first coming of Christ, how much more carefully should we be searching the New Testament to understand Jesus' second coming? And even more so since we may well be living in the days of His visible appearance!

Terms we should know that all speak of the same time frame

The Second Coming

The Return of the Lord

The Day of the Lord

The Day of Judgment

The End of the Age

The Rapture of the Church

The Day of God's Wrath

The Tribulation

The Great Tribulation

The tribulation period is a seven-year period of rule that starts with the 'man of peace' or Antichrist making a "covenant with many" (Daniel 9:27) and leads to rebuilding the Jewish temple.

The great tribulation is the second half of the tribulation, which is described in Revelation 11-13 as forty-two months, 1260 days, or 3½ years. This period will start with the "abomination that causes desolation", Matthew 24:15, and lead to a time of terror that the Earth has never seen before, nor will it ever see such again, Matthew 24:21. This all will be under the direction of the Antichrist.

Every single writer in the New Testament spoke of the end times and the literal return of Jesus Christ to the Earth. Nonetheless, due to issues that were cited in the last chapter, over time it became very easy to second-guess the simple truth taught in the Bible.

Four major observations in the New Testament that serve as a witness regarding the second coming of Jesus

We are going to see an amazingly cohesive, logical, and explainable timeline of events that lead up to the tribulation and eventually to the rapture of the church. Everything will be kept in context to avoid confusing language.

1. **What Jesus personally taught His own disciples about His return.** These lessons are recorded in the Gospels. This will be covered in the current chapter.

2. **What Jesus told the chief priest and religious leaders on the night He was betrayed.** We could call this His "legal testimony". Why? This is the testimony that Jesus gave to the Jewish high priest and the chief Jewish leaders regarding His second coming. It provided them the legal grounds to demand His death. It is this same testimony upon which our faith is based.

3. **The Apostle Paul's writings.** Because Paul was not one of the original twelve apostles, his perceptions were different. Paul had a strong influence on Luke's writing and wrote his own explanation of what **must** happen before Christ's return. This is an incredible testimony because it contradicts most of the teaching that the church has believed up to this point regarding the end times.

4. **The Book of Revelation** is clearly the least understood book of the Bible. The reason for this misunderstanding, I believe, is that we don't really understand and believe the first three points listed above. For that reason, only passages from Revelation that help to clarify the three previous observations will be cited.

It is important to understand that all four New Testament observations listed above are in absolute agreement. They represent one solid message of warning to the church today, and they make up the most important testimony in the Bible about Jesus' return.

Fifty or even one hundred years ago it was not as important for pastors and leaders to search out these things as it is today. Why? Those leaders were not living in the very days before Jesus' second coming.

Because of the critical moment in which we are living, believing a false narrative about Jesus' return is dangerous, not only for you personally, but also for the church. Your pastors and Bible school teachers of a previous generation may have been a bit sloppy on this subject, but we cannot afford this indulgence today.

Why? It will lead you and many of your family and friends to fall away from the Lord and take the mark of the beast.

The first warning that Jesus gave His disciples when they asked about His return was "*watch out that no one deceives you*". Matthew 24, Mark 13, and Luke 21.

The people most prone to deception are always those who believe that THEY cannot be deceived.

You will find that most misconceptions about Christ's return within current church consideration were developed as Bible teachers tried to make the teaching of Jesus' second coming fit into a distorted scenario. This is somewhat reasonable since it can be attributed to the absence of Israel and no Jewish temple. With Israel's reconstitution half of the puzzle has been solved, and the temple can be rebuilt as soon as a favorable political scenario presents itself. Clearly, the historic objections are no longer valid.

There is still no Jewish temple. One miraculous sign to come.

Just as Israel was restored as a national homeland for the Jewish people, the temple will be rebuilt! The point bears repeating. Just as Israel was restored as a national homeland for the Jewish people, the Jewish temple will be rebuilt! In fact, you will soon see that Jesus will return for the church shortly after the Jewish temple is rebuilt.

Let's look at the gospels of Matthew, Mark, and Luke.

The first observation…Jesus' teaching to His disciples.

When Jesus' disciples asked about His return, His specific teaching included the rapture of the church. His main teaching on these signs and His return can be found in Matthew 24, Mark 13, and Luke 21. Jesus lists deception as being a key issue. He continues with other general signs of His return which include the following:

- False prophets
- Wars and rumors of wars
- Nation against nation, kingdom against kingdom
- Famines, pestilence, and great earthquakes
- Persecution and hatred against believers
- Family betrayal
- False messiahs
- Increase in wickedness
- Many falling away from the faith
- Great signs from heaven and fearful natural events

As we look at this list, we can see that the only natural disasters are earthquakes, famines, pestilence, and possibly hurricanes. Everything else on the list is rooted in the sinful heart of man and the work of the sinister force of Satan, who "deceives the whole world" (Revelation 12:9). After reading the above list, you would have to agree that all of these signs have been occurring for the last 2,000 years and more.

The gospel of the kingdom preached in the whole world.

Matthew 24:14 *And this gospel of the kingdom will be preached in the whole world as a testimony to all nations, and then the end will come.*

This sign is different because preaching and publishing the gospel in every nation, includes thousands of people groups. It is a definite singular event that's becoming a reality as you read this. This prophecy points to a single time frame.

Missionaries have reached all but a very small percentage of the people groups on the planet. Using state-of-the-art technology, they are rapidly translating the written word of God for each people group. In fact, the process requires just a fraction of the time that it took a generation ago. Some translation methods can produce a localized version of the New Testament in just a few weeks!

Nonetheless, it will be virtually impossible for any Christian leader to proclaim, "Stop preaching, the job is finished!" Only God will know that with certainty.

What else did Matthew, Mark, and Luke record that would have to take place prior to Jesus' return?

Jesus lists specific signs that will occur only once in history, and they all must happen before the rapture of the church.

These signs cannot take place until there is a Jewish temple in Jerusalem. As mentioned, the Jewish temple is one of the key signs. Again, this is why scholars and Bible teachers had to create alternate scenarios for Jesus' return. At present it is quite plain that Jesus cannot return because there is no temple.

There is one key verse from the Old Testament that Jesus references in His specific end time teaching—it is Daniel 9:27 where Daniel is speaking about the Antichrist. Keep in mind the person of the Antichrist is called the beast in the book of Revelation.

Here's the passage Jesus refers to:

Daniel 9:27 *"He [the Antichrist] will confirm a covenant with many for one seven. In the middle of the seven he will put an end to sacrifice and offering. And **at the temple** he will set up an **abomination that causes desolation**, until the end that is decreed is poured out on him."*

Now Jesus' teaching. Notice what He emphasizes.

Matthew 24:15 *"So when you see standing in the holy place '**the abomination that causes desolation**,' spoken of through the prophet Daniel—let the reader understand—*

Matthew 24:15 will take place:
- **After** the Gospel is preached to every people group on the planet. Matthew 24:14
- **After** the Antichrist has already made the seven-year treaty, presumably a peace covenant with Israel.
- **After** the Jewish temple has been rebuilt.

- **After**, as indicated, the Jewish priests will be offering animal sacrifices at the temple.
- **After** the Antichrist breaks the seven-year covenant at the half- way point.

This break of the seven-year covenant will set in motion the great tribulation.

This will be followed by Christ's return and rapture of the church. Matthew 24:27-31

It is the making of the covenant that starts the seven-year tribulation. The violation of the agreement at the halfway point initiates the 3½ year time frame called the great tribulation.

Jesus refers to the great tribulation a few verses later.

Matthew 24:21 *For then {after the abomination] there will be great distress, unequaled from the beginning of the world until now—and never to be equaled again.*

The King James Bible and several of the older versions call it great tribulation.

Matthew 24:21 *For then shall be **great tribulation**, such as was not since the beginning of the world to this time, no, nor ever shall be.* KJB

The place we get tripped up is the verses between 24:15 "the abomination that causes desolation" and 24:21 great tribulation are these:

Matthew 24:16-20 *"then let those who are in Judea flee to the mountains. [17] Let no one on the housetop go down to take anything out of the house. [18] Let no one in the field go back to get their cloak. [19] How dreadful it will be in those days for pregnant women and nursing mothers! [20] Pray that your flight will not take place in winter or on the Sabbath."*

We can see that this passage above applies to people in Israel and Judea in particular. It is these people who will be immediately threated when the beast institutes the "abomination of desolation" because this all happens in Jerusalem. This is the abomination that begins the time of desolation or great tribulation, referred to in verse 21.

Verses 15–21 are all being released by one act. The beast, after 3½ years of charm and peace, suddenly believes he is God and demands worship. We will look carefully at the motive for his demand in 2 Thessalonians and Revelation. Keep in mind, the beast will pull off the greatest deception in all human history.

An essential and rudimentary question that must be asked is: What is the great distress or great tribulation about? As hinted at, the beast of Revelation will demand the worship of all people worldwide. He will use the force of legislative power to carry out his demand. Those who resist him and refuse to worship him as God will be put to death.

So then, those who worship him as God will receive the "mark of the beast", and those who resist will be hunted down and killed.

His followers will receive special economic and political benefits. His "mark" will give its recipient all of the access to marketplace that they always had as well as the ability to travel freely.

Remember that at this time the gospel will have been preached to every person, Matthew 24:14. So men are without excuse.

The beast will actually be used by God's sovereign plan to force every individual on the planet to choose between the God of love and the god of this age. The God who gave free will and the god who forces his will upon them. The God of eternity and the god of the immediate.

So the resistors will be red-flagged or locked out of the global economy. The choice will come to each person on the planet.

Christians who hold on to their faith will be on the run and under severe pressure. We will talk more about this in a later chapter.

The next verses in Matthew warn believers of the panic, confusion, and powerful deception that will come on those who try to hold out from worshipping the beast and taking his mark.

Matthew 24:23-27 *"At that time if anyone says to you, 'Look, here is the Messiah!' or, 'There he is!' do not believe it. 24 For false messiahs and false prophets will appear and perform great signs and wonders to deceive, if possible, even the elect. 25 See, I have told you ahead of time. 26 So if anyone tells you, 'There he is, out in the wilderness,' do not go out; or, 'Here he is, in the inner rooms,' do not believe it. 27 For as lightning that comes from the east is visible even in the west, so will be the coming of the Son of Man."*

Because the deception is so powerful and our choices are now eternal, God will send angelic messengers to those who refuse to worship the beast and are shut out of the economic system. During this time of great tribulation, God will warn Christ-believing resisters and nonbelieving holdouts who were ill-prepared to confront this season of intense challenge.

Revelation 14:6-12 "*Then I saw another angel flying in midair, and he had the eternal gospel to proclaim to those who live on the Earth—to every nation, tribe, language and people. 7 He said in a loud voice, 'Fear God and give him glory, because the hour of his judgment has come. Worship him who made the heavens, the Earth, the sea and the springs of water.'*

8 A second angel followed and said, 'Fallen! Fallen is Babylon the Great,' which made all the nations drink the maddening wine of her adulteries.

9 A third angel followed them and said in a loud voice: "If anyone worships the beast and its image and receives its mark on their forehead or on their hand, 10 they, too, will drink the wine of God's fury, which has been poured full strength into the cup of his wrath. They will be tormented with burning sulfur in the presence of the holy angels and of the Lamb. 11 And the smoke of their torment will rise for ever and ever. There will be no rest day or night for those who worship the beast and its image, or for anyone who receives the mark of its name." 12 This calls for patient endurance on the part of the people of God who keep his commands and remain faithful to Jesus."

Nowhere in the Bible does it say that Christians will be raptured before the great tribulation and Jesus' return.

In Matthew 24:29-31 Jesus makes it very clear that **after the distress of those days. What days?** The days of the great tribulation. Then there will be signs in the heavens, then His return, and then the rapture.

Matthew 24:29 *"Immediately after the distress of those days the sun will be darkened, and the moon will not give its light; the stars will fall from the sky, and the heavenly bodies will be shaken."*

Then, Jesus returns:

Matthew 24:30 *"**Then will appear** the sign of the Son of Man in heaven. And then all the peoples of the Earth will mourn when they see the Son of Man coming on the clouds of heaven, with power and great glory."*

Then, and only then, does the rapture of the church occur.

Matthew 24:31 *"**And he will send his angels with a loud trumpet call, and they will gather his elect from the four winds**, from one end of the heavens to the other."*

Jesus's Timeline again from Matthew 24—Five Precise Predictions in Order

1. Verse 15...*So **when** you see standing in the holy place 'the abomination that causes desolation', spoken of through the prophet Daniel—let the reader understand—*

2. Verse 21...*For **then** there will be great distress, unequaled from the beginning of the world until now—and never to be equaled again.*

3. Verse 29..."*Immediately **after** the distress of those days" 'the sun will be darkened, and the moon will not give its light; the stars will fall from the sky and the heavenly bodies will be shaken'.*

4. Verse 30..."***Then** will appear the sign of the Son of Man in heaven. And then all the peoples of the Earth will mourn when they see the Son of Man coming on the clouds of heaven, with power and great glory."*

5. Verse 31...*And **he will send** his angels with a loud trumpet call, and they will gather his elect from the four winds, from one end of the heavens to the other.*

Earlier in this chapter we covered the general signs of the last days from Matthew 24, Mark 13, and Luke 21. We will look next at the almost identical, word for word, narration and timeline in Mark's gospel which includes the same warnings about deception as well as the same general signs.

Mark 13:14-27 "**When you see 'the abomination that causes desolation'** *standing where it does not belong—let the reader understand—then let those who are in Judea flee to the mountains.* [15] *Let no one on the housetop go down or enter the house to take anything out.* [16] *Let no one in the field go back to get their cloak.* [17] *How dreadful it will be in those days for pregnant women and nursing mothers!* [18] *Pray that this will not take place in winter,* [19] **because those will be days of distress unequaled** *from the beginning, when God created the world, until now—and never to be equaled again.* [20] "*If the Lord had not cut short those days, [to 3½ years] no one would survive. But for the sake of the elect, whom he has chosen, he has shortened them.* [21] *At that time if anyone says to you, 'Look, here is the Messiah!' or, 'Look, there he is!' do not believe it.* [22] *For false messiahs and false prophets will appear and perform signs and wonders to deceive, if possible, even the elect.* [23] *So be on your guard; I have told you everything ahead of time.* [24] **But in those days, following that distress,** *the 'sun will be darkened, and the moon will not give its light;* [25] *the stars will fall from the sky, and the heavenly bodies will be shaken.'* [26] "**At that time people will see the Son of Man coming in clouds** *with great power and glory.* [27] **And he**

will send his angels and gather his elect *from the four winds, from the ends of the Earth to the ends of the heavens.*

Jesus' Timeline in Mark 13—Five Precise Predictions in Order

1. Verse 14...**When you see** 'the abomination that causes desolation' standing where it does not belong—let the reader understand—

2. Verse 19...**because those will be days of distress unequalled** from the beginning, when God created the world, until now and never to be equaled again.

3. Verse 24...But in those days, **following that distress,**

4. Verse 26...**At that time** people will see...the Son of Man coming in the clouds

5. Verse 27...And **He will send his angels** and gather his elect from the four winds, from the ends of the Earth...

Luke 21 – The language in Luke is just a bit different from Matthew and Mark. This can be attributed to the fact that Luke's audience was primarily Gentile while Matthew and Mark designed their texts primarily for a Jewish audience. Therefore, Luke was less reliant on Daniel's specific prophecy. Significantly, the sequence of events is identical and can be followed easily.

Luke 21:20 When you see Jerusalem being surrounded by armies, you will know that its desolation is near. *(See Matthew 24:15, Mark 13:14)* *21 Then let those who are in Judea flee to the mountains, let those in the city get out, and let those in the country not enter the city. 22 For this is the time of punishment in fulfillment of all that has been written. 23 How dreadful it will be in those days for pregnant women and nursing mothers!* **There will be great distress [great tribulation] in the land and wrath against this people.** *24 They will fall by the sword and will be taken as prisoners to all the nations.* **Jerusalem will be trampled on by the Gentiles until the times of the Gentiles are fulfilled. [for forty-two months or 3½ years Revelation 11:2]** *25 "There will be signs in the sun, moon and stars. On the Earth, nations will be in anguish and perplexity at the roaring and tossing of the sea. 26 People will faint from terror, apprehensive of what is coming on the world, for the heavenly bodies will be shaken.* **27 At that time they will see the Son of Man coming in a cloud with power and great glory. 28 When these things begin to take place, stand up and lift up your heads, because your redemption is drawing near.** *[The rapture of the church is at hand.]*

1. Verse 20...*When you see Jerusalem being surrounded by armies, you will know that its desolation **[abomination of desolation]** is near.*

2. Verse 23...**There will be great distress in the land [great tribulation]**

3. Verse 24...**Jerusalem will be trampled on by the Gentiles until the times of the Gentiles are fulfilled. [42 months or 3½ years]**

4. Verse 27...**At that time they will see the Son of Man coming in a cloud with power and great glory.**

5. Verse 28...**When these things begin to take place, stand up and lift up your heads, because your redemption is drawing near. [Rapture of church]**

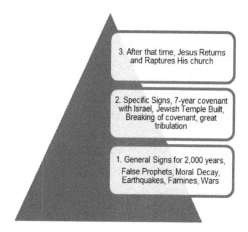

3. After that time, Jesus Returns and Raptures His church

2. Specific Signs, 7-year covenant with Israel, Jewish Temple Built, Breaking of covenant, great tribulation

1. General Signs for 2,000 years, False Prophets, Moral Decay, Earthquakes, Famines, Wars

As you can see, all of Jesus' teachings in Matthew, Mark, and Luke follow this pattern. In the next chapter we will see what Paul the Apostle taught on this subject

Revelation 4:1-6

After this I looked, and there before me was a door standing open in heaven. And the voice I had first heard speaking to me like a trumpet said, "Come up here, and I will show you what must take place after this." 2 At once I was in the Spirit, and there before me was a throne in heaven with someone sitting on it. 3 And the one who sat there had the appearance of jasper and ruby. A rainbow that shone like an emerald encircled the throne. 4 Surrounding the throne were twenty-four other thrones, and seated on them were twenty-four elders. They were dressed in white and had crowns of gold on their heads. 5 From the throne came flashes of lightning, rumblings and peals of thunder. In front of the throne, seven lamps were blazing. These are the seven spirits of God. 6 Also in front of the throne there was what looked like a sea of glass, clear as crystal.

4

THE TESTIMONY OF JESUS IS THE SPIRIT OF PROPHECY

The testimony that Jesus gave to the high priest of Israel on the night that He was betrayed was a binding, sworn legal testimony. It was this witness that gave the high priest and his cohorts the legal authority to have Jesus condemned and crucified by the Roman government.

Why is this testimony important to us now and in the dark days to come?

- This is the central truth of the New Testament that we must accept. Jesus is the Christ, the Son of God, and He is coming back in the clouds to judge the Earth and save His people.

- It is the central hope that we must hold on to. The book of Revelation starts with the "testimony of Jesus" in Revelation 1:2 and ends with the "testimony of Jesus" in Revelation 22:16.

- It is this testimony that will make us enemies of the world and of the beast. Ultimately, it will lead to martyrdom for some, and perhaps many.

- Finally, **this testimony is the spirit of prophecy** and separates those operating in the office of the prophet from those with a prophetic gifting or words of knowledge.

In addition to Jesus' definitive teaching to His twelve apostles on His second coming, it is important that we look at what Jesus stated before He was crucified. These are not the famous "seven last sayings of Christ" that He gave while in the process of being crucified, but rather a private conversation that Jesus shared with Israel's chief priest and his trusted inner circle.

During this exchange recorded in both Mark 14 and Luke 22, the word that the Jewish leaders used was "testimony". This word in the Greek it is *martyrian*. Bible scholars define *martyrian* as "judicial or legal testimony" given in court.

Keep this in mind because *martyrian* is used eight times in Revelation and always in a heroic sense. Frequently, those who "hold on to the testimony" during persecution are martyred in the process.

It is this final testimony that Jesus gave to the Jewish leaders that caused Him to be found guilty of the great sin of blasphemy.

In the testimony that was given at His trial face to face with Israel's high priest and chief religious leaders, He prophesied about His return, or His second coming. Again, this is what gave the authorities grounds to demand Jesus' execution. Their charge? Blasphemy! They asked Jesus if He was in fact the Messiah.

What did Jesus say?

Matthew 26:63-66 *63bThe high priest said to him, "I charge you under oath by the living God: Tell us if you are the Messiah (the Christ), the Son of God." 64 "You have said so," Jesus replied. "But I say* *to all of you: From now on you will see the Son of Man sitting at the right hand of the Mighty One and coming on the clouds of heaven."* **65** *Then the high priest tore his clothes and said, "He has spoken blasphemy! Why do we need any more witnesses? Look, now you have heard the blasphemy.* **66** *What do you think? 'He is worthy of death,'' they answered.*

Jesus, by declaring Himself to be the Jewish Messiah, was declaring to them, "I am God in the flesh." The Jewish leaders simply could not comprehend a lamb-like Messiah.

If Jesus' statement to them of His return sounds a familiar, you can refresh your memory by reviewing chapter two. He is telling us what His appearance will look like at His second coming.

Declaring His bodily return to Earth as the Son of God gave the Jewish leaders justification for the crucifixion!

Mark 14:61-64 **61b** *"Again the high priest asked him, "Are you the Messiah, the Son of the Blessed One?"* **62** *"I am," said Jesus. "And you will see the Son of Man sitting at the right hand of the Mighty One and coming on the clouds of heaven".* **63** *The high priest tore his clothes. "Why do we need any more witnesses?" he asked.* **64** *"You* have heard the blasphemy. What do you think?" They all condemned him as worthy of death.

Here is Luke's version of the events:

Luke 22:66-71 *At daybreak the council of the elders of the people, both the chief priests and the teachers of the law, met together, and Jesus was led before them.* **67** *"If you are the Messiah," they said, "tell us." Jesus answered, "If I tell you, you will not believe me,* **68** *and if I asked you, you would not answer.* **69** *But from now on,* **the Son of Man will be seated at the right hand of the mighty God."** **70** *They all asked, "Are you then the Son of God?" He replied, "You say that I am."* **71** *Then they said, "Why do we need any more testimony? We have heard it from his own lips."*

These leaders had been listening for three years and wanted to hear Jesus tell them plainly who He was. He would not tell them until they had already made up their minds to kill Him. Perhaps at the beginning of His ministry Jesus could have sat down with them and explained His plan and purpose, but that was not God's will. Jesus came for this very purpose of being slain for the sins of the world.

His sudden and straightforward confession that they would see Him "sitting at the right hand of the mighty God" and "coming on the clouds of heaven" was His declaration that He was equal with God! Jesus was quoting a Messianic text from the book of Daniel which paints the picture of the Messiah that they were expecting.

Daniel 7:13-14 *In my vision at night I looked, and there before me was **one like a son of man, coming with the clouds of heaven.** He approached the Ancient of Days and was led into his presence. ¹⁴ **He was given authority, glory and sovereign power; all nations and peoples of every language worshiped him. His dominion is an everlasting dominion that will not pass away, and his kingdom is one that will never be destroyed.** (Emphasis mine.)*

Jesus boldly declared Himself to be the Messiah according to the Daniel 7 description. This was equivalent to saying that He was equal with God, and this is why he was charged with and condemned of blasphemy. Of course, Jesus was only telling the truth. Yet, for that same reason, He was executed because the Jewish hierarchy simply was unwilling to fathom a Messiah such as Jesus.

Leviticus 24:16 *Anyone who blasphemes the name of the* LORD *is to be put to death. The entire assembly must stone them. Whether foreigner or native-born, when they blaspheme the Name they are to be put to death.*

The Jewish leaders were waiting for the opportunity to capture and kill Jesus, and what charge against him would be better than Jesus declaring Himself to be equal with God? To these leaders, Jesus did not fulfill their pet scripture passage, Daniel 7. Instead, He conformed to passages that talked about a meek, suffering servant Messiah such as Isaiah 53:4-7. Jesus is in fact both the suffering Messiah of Isaiah 53 and the powerful, conquering Messiah of Daniel 7. Jesus will reveal His Daniel 7 power when He returns for us.

What does the testimony of Jesus mean to us today?

The following passages in Revelation speak of the testimony of Jesus:

Revelation 1:1-2 *¹ The revelation from Jesus Christ, which God gave him to show his servants what must soon take place. He made it known by sending his angel to his servant John, ² who testifies to* everything he saw—that is, the word of God and the **testimony** of Jesus Christ.

Revelation 1:9 *I, John, your brother and companion in the suffering and kingdom and patient endurance that are ours in Jesus, was on the island of Patmos because of the word of God and the **testimony** of Jesus.*

Revelation 6:9 *When he opened the fifth seal, I saw under the altar the souls of those who had been slain because of the word of God and the **testimony** they had maintained.*

Revelation 11:7 *Now when they have finished their **testimony**, the beast that comes up from the Abyss will attack them, and overpower and kill them.*

Revelation 12:9 *They triumphed over him by the blood of the Lamb and by the word of their **testimony**; they did not love their lives so much as to shrink from death.*

Revelation 12:17 *Then the dragon was enraged at the woman and went off to wage war against the rest of her offspring—those who keep God's commands and hold fast their **testimony** about Jesus.*

Revelation 17:6 *I saw that the woman was drunk with the blood of God's holy people, the blood of those who bore* **testimony** *to Jesus. When I saw her, I was greatly astonished.*

Revelation 19:10 *At this I fell at his feet to worship him. But he said to me, "Don't do that! I am a fellow servant with you and with your brothers and sisters who hold to the* **testimony** *of Jesus. Worship God! For it is the Spirit of prophecy who bears* **testimony** *to Jesus."*

Revelation 20:4 *I saw thrones on which were seated those who had been given authority to judge. And I saw the souls of those who had been beheaded because of their* **testimony** *about Jesus and because of the word of God. They had not worshiped the beast or its image and had not received its mark on their foreheads or their hands. They came to life and reigned with Christ a thousand years.*

Revelation 22:16 *"I, Jesus, have sent my angel to give you this* **testimony** *for the churches. I am the Root and the Offspring of David, and the bright Morning Star."*

5

THE WITNESS OF PAUL, THE APOSTLE, BORN OUT OF TIME: PART I

Paul differed from the original twelve apostles in that he was called to Jesus after the resurrection, after Pentecost, and during the explosive growth of the Jerusalem church. Paul describes his life like this:

Philippians 3:5-8 *Circumcised on the eighth day, of the people of Israel, of the tribe of Benjamin, a Hebrew of Hebrews; in regard to the law, a Pharisee; ⁶ as for zeal, persecuting the church; as for righteousness based on the law, faultless. ⁷ But whatever were gains to me I now consider loss for the sake of Christ. ⁸ What is more, I consider everything a loss because of the surpassing worth of knowing Christ Jesus my Lord, for whose sake I have lost all things. I consider them garbage that I may gain Christ…"*

In Acts 7, we find Paul guarding the coats of those who stone Stephen to death as he proclaims the gospel message. Paul was part of the persecution that shook the growing church in Jerusalem. A bit later, Paul is converted while on the road to Damascus with plans to crush the church. His transformation is the result of a personal encounter with Jesus.

Acts 9:1-5 *Meanwhile, Saul was still breathing out murderous threats against the Lord's disciples. He went to the high priest 2 and asked him for letters to the synagogues in Damascus, so that if he found any there who belonged to the Way, whether men or women, he might take them as prisoners to Jerusalem. 3 As he neared Damascus on his journey, suddenly a light from heaven flashed around him. 4 He fell to the ground and heard a voice say to him, "Saul, Saul, why do you persecute me?" 5 "Who are you, Lord?" Saul asked. "I am Jesus, whom you are persecuting," he replied.*

Paul was quickly converted and over time received great revelations from the Lord. He wrote much of the New Testament, from the book of Romans to the book of Philemon. Many contend that he wrote Hebrews as well.

Not only did Paul write prolifically, but also, he was deeply influential in Luke's life. Luke was one of Paul's key disciples and wrote the gospel of Luke as well as the book of Acts.

Paul was quite bold. He had a degree of courage, persistence, and tenaciousness that is extremely rare. His powerful personality was driven by his love for Christ, the church, and the Jewish people.

Paul was persecuted and faced many brutal beatings. It is hard to imagine that any human being could suffer so severely and so frequently without backing down and either resigning or at least drastically toning down his message. Paul described to the Corinthians what he had faced for his faith:

2 Corinthians 11:24-27 *"Five times I received from the Jews the forty lashes minus one 25 Three times I was beaten with rods, once I was pelted with stones, three times I was shipwrecked, I spent a night and a day in the open sea, 26 I have been constantly on the move. I have been in danger from rivers, in danger from bandits, in danger from my fellow Jews, in danger from Gentiles; in danger in the city, in danger in the country, in danger at sea; and in danger from false believers. 27 I have labored and toiled and have often gone without sleep; I have known hunger and thirst and have often gone without food; I have been cold and naked."*

Many can just gloss over a passage like this without being affected. I cannot. Paul's testimony describes "*five times receiving from the Jews the forty lashes minus one*". In the ancient world this punishment was administered publicly as a warning to others. The

Jewish leaders would mete out thirty-nine lashes with a leather whip across the back. Forty lashes was considered a death sentence.

This was considered the maximum sentence. Perilously close to the death sentence, its intent was to break a man's will and to bring about a change of heart. How many church leaders do you know who would keep preaching after one public beating of the thirty-nine lashes on their bare backs by an angry adversary? I fear that I might cave in under this kind of beating.

Paul suffered this public and painful humiliation five times. He was beaten with rods on three separate occasions. It is hard to believe that this was a real man and not a superhero with a halo.

If you have ever seen a video of the "caning" that is still done in Singapore or Malaysia, it will give you an idea what it was like for Paul to be beaten with rods. It is a punishment so severe that welts appear with the first strike and the skin breaks with the second or third strike. A few more strikes leave the person brutalized and bloody. On three separate occasions he was beaten with rods.

Paul was also stoned and left for dead. This too was a form of capital punishment.

I can't think of anyone else in church history whose suffering for the gospel would compare to Paul's. Tradition says his suffering finally ended around 64-67 AD in Rome when he was beheaded.

Paul sets the bar very high for anyone who wants to call himself an apostle in this age. It is also impossible to believe that a man this committed and this stubborn would give mixed signals to the church about the very important issue concerning the return of Jesus. Significantly, this was the very reason he was beaten repeatedly—for "proclaiming the resurrection of Christ, and the coming judgment".

The Secret Rapture

Paul's writings in his first letter to the Thessalonian church in which he spoke about the return of Christ is one of the passages that is used **out of context** for those promoting a secret rapture of the church. Another passage used out of context is found in I Corinthians 15.

The notion of a pre-tribulation, secret rapture of the church originated and was propagated by John Darby in the 1830s and again by Cyrus Ingerson Scofield in the 1880s. Each of these men wrote his own Bible translation and study notes to spread their popular message of a pre-tribulation rapture of the church. They also became very wealthy teaching this appealing message. The deception they taught was that Jesus raptures us before the tribulation so that we never have to suffer. It's a grave error in Bible translation.

In many countries around the world this teaching is laughable. Christians in China, Russia, Cuba, Vietnam, North Korea, India, and Iran, among others, suffer persecution on a regular basis. They suffer loss of work and loss of possessions, beatings, imprisonment and even death for the gospel.

Pre-Tribulation Timeline

Darby and Scofield taught that the secret rapture must happen before the appearance of the Antichrist and his seven-year covenant. They taught the rapture would occur prior to the Jewish temple being rebuilt by the Antichrist and before the abomination that causes desolation takes place.

Since there was no Israel at the time that Darby and Scofield lived, their teaching seemed very plausible. Over time, Christian leaders and prominent individuals accepted this new doctrine as fact. There are at least two large church denominations in the United States that include accepting this doctrine as a precondition for ordination.

However, this doctrine is a direct contradiction to what Jesus shows us in His teachings. When we read through the gospels of Matthew, Mark, and Luke, we can see that each gospel adheres to the same timeline for Jesus' return.

This leads to a logical question: Did Paul have a new revelation that differed from what Jesus taught? Would the Father allow Jesus to lie in the gospels, or do teachers of the pre-tribulation doctrine take the teachings of Paul out of context?

Fake News?

We see a lot of false reporting in the news today. It could be called disinformation, we call it fake news. Is it possible that over the 2,000 years of church history Satan has influenced several prominent teachers to disseminate a theory rather than authentic

Bible doctrine and, in this way, weaken the church at the end of this age? If so, much of the church is living under a false hope!

We will take a look at the first passage of Paul's that is taken out of context.

1 Corinthians 15:51 *Listen, I tell you a mystery: We will not all sleep, but we will all be changed—* **52** *in a flash, in the twinkling of an eye,* ***at the last trumpet****. For the* ***trumpet will sound****, the* ***dead will be raised*** *imperishable, and we will be changed.*

In 1 Corinthians 15, Paul teaches on the resurrection body for fifty verses, not on the timing of Christ's return. Nevertheless, Paul does give a hint as to the timing of Christ's return when he states, **"in a flash**...and **at the last trumpet, for the trumpet will sound, the dead will be raised"**.

So, we can conclude the following: The last trumpet will sound, then the rapture will take place, and we will be changed in a "flash". Pay attention to the context. It is "at the last trumpet". The return of the Lord does not happen in a vacuum. How did Jesus describe His return?

Luke 17:24 *For the Son of Man in his day* **will be like the lightning, which flashes and lights up the sky** *from one end to the other.*

Matthew 24:31 *And he will send his angels* **with a loud trumpet call**, *and they will gather his elect from the four winds, from one end of the heavens to the other.*

These are previews of the Lord's return to Earth, which include Revelation 11.

Revelation 11:15 *The seventh angel sounded his trumpet, and there were loud voices in heaven, which said: "The kingdom of the world has become the kingdom of our Lord and of his Messiah, and he will reign for ever and ever."*

As those who believe that we are living in the last days, we must be on the lookout for false prophets and teachers. We find these warnings in Matthew 24, Mark 13, and Luke 21, as well as 2 Thessalonians 2, 1 John, and Revelation.

Just how do we develop discernment? You must get alone with God every day and begin reading the Bible for your own benefit. As you study and receive support from the Holy Spirit, you will begin to gain discernment. The more you handle the truth, the easier it is to detect the counterfeit.

When a teacher or a pastor makes a statement that seems a bit off, you can inquire of the Lord about it. Prayerfully read the context of the passage that you believe was misquoted and grow in your role as a student of God's word. What this means is that we are responsible for what we hear and how we apply it.

Here is the next passage by Paul that is frequently cited out of context.

I Thessalonians 4:15 *According to the Lord's word, we tell you that we who are still alive, who are left until the coming of the Lord, will certainly not precede those who have fallen asleep. 16 For the Lord himself will come down from heaven, with a **loud command**, with **the voice of the archangel** and with **the trumpet call of God**, and the dead in Christ will rise first. 17 After that, we who are still alive and are left will be caught up together with them in the clouds to meet the Lord in the air. And so we will be with the Lord forever.*

Paul, in this passage, is giving assurance to the church that those who believed and passed away will be the first ones raised up when the Lord comes back. Paul is not teaching a timeline about when the Lord is coming, only that "the dead in Christ will be raised first." In this passage, he also gives us enough facts so that we can know that the rapture will in no way be secret.

There is enough detail in this short passage to tell us that the rapture of the church will be thunderous and visually exhilarating for believers.

- **The Lord comes down** from heaven
- With a **loud command**
- With **the voice of an archangel**
- With **the trumpet call of God -** Trumpets were used in the Bible as a public alert system!
- We will be caught up together with them [believers who had passed on earlier] in the clouds to **meet the Lord in the air.**

Again, Paul makes it clear that the rapture of the church will be very visible and very loud. Things don't get much louder than "the trumpet call of God". **By no means will this be hush-hush!** The Lord will descend from heaven and we will be caught up in the air.

Paul continues in his letter to the Thessalonians:

1 Thessalonians 5:1-6 *Now, brothers and sisters, about times and dates we do not need to write to you, ² for you know very well that the day of the Lord will come like a thief in the night. ³ While people are saying, "Peace and safety," destruction will come on them suddenly, as labor pains on a pregnant woman, and they will not escape.*

⁴ But you, brothers and sisters, are not in darkness so that this day should surprise you like a thief. ⁵ You are all children of the light and children of the day. We do not belong to the night or to the darkness. ⁶ So then, let us not be like others, who are asleep, but let us be awake and sober.

I mentioned before that much of the church will become disillusioned and offended; many will fall away altogether.

Paul says <u>we will not be surprised</u> as if by a thief; he instructs us to stay awake and sober. This is very clear, but apparently some of Paul's readers were confused. Therefore, the apostle addresses the subject more forcefully in 2 Thessalonians

Revelation 1:7-8

"Look, he is coming with the clouds,"

and "every eye will see him,

even those who pierced him";

and all peoples on earth "will mourn because of him."

So shall it be! Amen.

8 "I am the Alpha and the Omega," says the Lord God, "who is, and

who was, and who is to come, the Almighty."

6

THE WITNESS OF PAUL: PART 2

2 Thessalonians

There is enough material in chapters 1 and 2 of 2 Thessalonians to write an entire book dealing with the subject of the Lord's return. We ought to read them over and over.

In this chapter we will focus mostly on the issue of timing.

In Paul's first letter to the Thessalonians, he made it clear that the prepared church would be well aware of the timeline leading up to the Lord's loud and visible return. Just in case they forgot about his first visit, Paul reminds them of the details that he taught them previously.

2 Thessalonians 2:5 *Don't you remember that when I was with you, I used to tell you these things?*

Keep in mind that we know from Acts 17:1-2 that Paul was only in Thessalonica for three sabbaths—that's three weeks of preaching, converting, baptizing and discipling. Look at what Paul is reminding this brand-new church, full of baby Christians, when he writes his second letter.

What things?

Did Paul try to soften the blow concerning what to expect about Christ's return? Did he try to avoid or water down the message of the dark times that were coming to the world before Christ's return?

After his introduction in 2 Thessalonians 1, Paul focuses specifically on the subject of Christ's return.

2 Thessalonians 1:6-10 *God is just: He will pay back trouble to those who trouble you ⁷ and give relief to you who are troubled, and to us as well. This will happen when the Lord Jesus is revealed from heaven in blazing fire with his powerful angels. ⁸ He will punish those who do not know God and do not obey the gospel of our Lord Jesus. ⁹ They will be punished with everlasting destruction and shut out from the presence of the Lord and from the glory of his might ¹⁰* **on the day he comes to be glorified in his holy people and to be marveled at among all those who have believed.** *This includes you, because you believed our testimony to you.*

Paul is speaking of the rapture: *"the day that he comes to be glorified in his holy people"*.

In chapter one, Paul told the church that Jesus is coming back for a reason—*"to be glorified in His holy people and **to be marveled at among all those who have believed"***.

The Greek term for "marveled' used here is *thaumazo*, which means "to be amazed (at), in wonder, astonished, surprised" (*Mounce's Greek*). The word is used forty-three times in the New Testament and connotes seeing or hearing something amazing.

Jesus marveled people with His words in the Gospels. What will it be like when He lights up the pitch-black sky in His full glory and splendor when He leaves His Father's right hand with all of the heavenly host during His return?

Matthew 24:29 *"the sun will be darkened, and the moon will not give its light; the stars will fall from the sky, and the heavenly bodies will be shaken."*

This verse seems to indicate that immediately prior to Jesus' return, the sky will go black, and then Christ will appear with trumpets, the command of heaven, and the shout of the archangel. This will be an event completely without precedent!

Matthew 24:30-31 *Then will appear the sign of the Son of Man in heaven. And then all the peoples of the Earth will mourn when they see the Son of Man coming on the clouds of heaven, with power and great glory.*

31 And he will send his angels with a loud trumpet call, and they will gather his elect from the four winds, from one end of the heavens to the other.

This appearing includes the rapture of saints.

Jesus is coming to amaze His people with His power, beauty and splendor. Jesus will be center stage and seen by all. Why does the world mourn? **They mourn because** they did not believe the message and they did not prepare for His coming.

Paul ends 2 Thessalonians 1 with a prayer and encouragement, and then he goes right back to the subject of Jesus' second coming in chapter two.

Now let's take five minutes here so that you can read the first twelve verses of 2 Thessalonians 2. Then we will have some comments.

2 Thessalonians 2:1-12

Concerning the coming of our Lord Jesus Christ and our being gathered to him, we ask you, brothers and sisters,

2 not to become easily unsettled or alarmed by the teaching allegedly from us—whether by a prophecy or by word of mouth or by letter—asserting that the day of the Lord has already come.

3 Don't let anyone deceive you in any way, for that day will not come until the rebellion occurs and the man of lawlessness (the beast) is revealed, the man doomed to destruction.

4 He will oppose and will exalt himself over everything that is called God or is worshiped, so that he sets himself up in God's temple, proclaiming himself to be God.

5 Don't you remember that when I was with you, I used to tell you these things?

6 And now you know what is holding him back, so that he may be revealed at the proper time.

7 For the secret power of lawlessness is already at work; but the one who now holds it back will continue to do so till he is taken out of the way.

8 And then the lawless one will be revealed, whom the Lord Jesus will overthrow with the breath of his mouth and destroy by the splendor of his coming.

9 The coming of the lawless one will be in accordance with how Satan works. He will use all sorts of displays of power through signs and wonders that serve the lie,

10 and all the ways that wickedness deceives those who are perishing. They perish because they refused to love the truth and so be saved.

11 For this reason God sends them a powerful delusion so that they will believe the lie

12 and so that all will be condemned who have not believed the truth but have delighted in wickedness.

Notice verse 1, where Paul says, *"Concerning **the coming of our Lord** Jesus Christ and **our being gathered to him.**"* Paul says clearly that first there will be the "coming of the Lord," followed by "our being gathered to him." This is synonymous with the rapture of the church.

Previously, I explained how the rapture immediately follows Jesus' return. These two events are so intertwined that they could almost be seen as a single global event.

Paul warned about those who believe or teach that *"the day of the Lord has already come."* Based on what Jesus taught, what Paul taught, and from what we know of history, we can state definitively *"The day of the Lord"* has NOT come.

It's troubling that today some are teaching that the Lord has returned and that we are living on Earth in the Millennial Kingdom now. This is another pathway to confusion regarding Jesus' return. Why do people believe this?

These teachers believe that the 70 AD destruction of the temple was the day of the Lord. They also believe that all of the prophecy concerning Jesus' second coming is fulfilled and that the book of Revelation is symbolic. This is a dangerous teaching.

Many thousands of Jewish people in Israel were killed in that revolt against Rome.

However, Jesus never appeared in the clouds and in glory for all to see. He never raptured His church and took vengeance on His enemies. He certainly did not fulfill the following passage that we looked at already—**Matthew 24:21** *"For then there will be great distress, unequaled from the beginning of the world until now—and never to be equaled again."*

Unquestionably, 70 AD was a time of immense distress. According to the renowned historian Josephus, approximately 1.1

million Jews died during that horrible time. However, during the World War II holocaust, at least six million Jewish people were slaughtered along with forty-six million others. Clearly the events of 70 AD did not fulfill the prophecy in Matthew 24:21.

Paul's topic here was very clear. "*Concerning the coming of our Lord Jesus Christ.*" Paul was asking them to "*not to become easily unsettled or alarmed by the teaching allegedly from us (his team)—whether by a prophecy or by word of mouth or by letter*".

Verse 2. "*not to become easily unsettled or alarmed by the teaching allegedly from us…*"

Jesus and Paul, along with every New Testament writer, warned us about false prophets and false teachers and their teachings directly preceding Jesus' return. This should be clear to you at this point.

A word about false prophets and false teachers.

I have watched many ministers up close over the years. False prophets are colorful; they carry a certain mystique. They give their words with a "God told me," "God said to me," "an angel visited me," or "I saw in a vision". I am not downgrading true prophets, but they will have the word of God. God's word points to His Son Jesus and His second coming. These leaders will be free of hype; they will not be peddling the gospel and splashing their pictures everywhere.

False teachers are different than false prophets in that they are more educated and refined. They will use Bible verses, Greek, Hebrew, and commentaries to support their teaching. Yet, when speaking of the weighty things of scripture such as suffering, persecution, and the second coming, they will either mislead or avoid the subject altogether. They may be sincere, but they will have very little prayer, call few prayer meetings, and fight to keep from hurting feelings.

Paul says the Lord will <u>not</u> come until...

Observe how Paul's next words align with Jesus' teaching and with what was recorded in the Gospels:

2 Thessalonians 2:3 *Don't let anyone deceive you in any way, for that day will not come until the rebellion occurs and the man of lawlessness is revealed, the man doomed to destruction.*

The rebellion that Paul mentions is the moral decay and radical turning from the true God and turning toward false teaching. Jesus warned about deception that is walking hand in hand with this falling away.

Matthew 24:10-12 *At that time many will turn away from the faith and will betray and hate each other,* 11 *and many false prophets will appear and deceive many people.* 12 *Because of the increase of wickedness, the love of most will grow cold,*

Next,

2 Thessalonians 2:4 *He will oppose and will exalt himself over everything that is called God or is worshiped, so that he sets himself up in God's temple, proclaiming himself to be God.*

Paul is describing here the person of the Antichrist, known also as the man of lawlessness and the beast.

This is the key sign that Jesus provided for us, and I cannot overemphasize this point. This act by the beast will shift the gears in heaven and on Earth from the tribulation period to the forty-two-month great tribulation. This action is the fulfillment of Daniel 9:27, Matthew 25:15, Mark 13:14, and Revelation 13:14-16.

The false god is the beast of Revelation. He will sit in the rebuilt Jewish temple and claim to be God! We also know from Revelation 13:15 that the beast will demand to be worshiped and those who refuse will be put to death. His followers will take his mark. Those who refuse to do so will be put to death. People who evade death will be imprisoned or live their lives as fugitives, unable to buy or sell.

Both Paul and Jesus warn us that we can be deceived easily on this subject.

This is exactly what Jesus said at the beginning of His teaching concerning the end of the age in Matthew 24:4-5: *"Do not let anyone deceive you. For many will come in my name, claiming, 'I am the Messiah' and will deceive many.*

In the USA, we have over 350,000 churches and pastors. There are almost as many para-church groups with their leaders. I believe the vast majority of these leaders are great, well-meaning people. They come in Jesus' name, claiming that He is the Christ, the Messiah, and many millions are deceived on this subject.

How do you know that I am not deceived as well? I could be way off. I only ask you to look carefully at these key passages and see if they are in context to the rest of the New Testament.

Why does the Bible give so much warning about deception during this time? We looked at the "confusion" that already exists on this subject.

In 2 Thessalonians 2:5, Paul says, "Don't you remember that when I was with you, I used to tell you these things?"

Today millions of believers either believe that Jesus came already in 70 AD or that He will come at any moment during a secret rapture. These teachings did not come from Jesus, Paul, or any other New Testament writer. Yet they are the only two theories accepted by the modern church and they are opposed to each other. [1]

When Jesus warned about deception, He was talking to the church that will face the anger of the post-Christian world that we are facing today. What's worse is that those who refuse to believe the truth will fall prey to the full force of Satan's deception and God's delusion.

Paul says in verses 2 Thessalonians 2:10b-12 "...*They perish because* **they refused to love the truth** *and so be saved.* [11] **For this reason God sends them a powerful delusion** *so that they will believe the* lie [12] *and so that all will be condemned who have not believed the truth but have delighted in wickedness."*

While we can see the rebellion against God occurring already in the world, it will grow visibly stronger as the "*man of lawlessness is revealed*". This is the beast of Revelation 13.

Jesus described this rebellion in **Matthew 24:10-12** *"At that time many will turn away from the faith and will betray and hate each other, [11] and many false prophets will appear and deceive many people. [12] Because of the increase of wickedness, the love of most will grow cold…"*

What brings on this rebellion? We will give reasons for this in further chapters; for the moment I want you to grasp the timing of Christ's return. **It is at the conclusion of the seven-year tribulation period.**

Paul also provides revelation about the "abomination that causes desolation" of whom both Daniel and Jesus spoke. The Jews and many unprepared Christians will begin to view him as the long-awaited Jewish Messiah. In fact, likely he will become so popular that the world begins to view him as a global savior.

Again, it is worth repeating…in **2 Thessalonians 2:3**, Paul says that Jesus will not come until *this* happens: "*for that day will not* come **until** the rebellion occurs and the man of lawlessness is revealed, the man doomed to destruction. Furthermore, Paul adds that, " *⁴He will oppose and will exalt himself over everything that is called God or is worshiped, so that he sets himself up in God's temple, proclaiming himself to be God.*"

So, from my point of view in 2019, what are the events that must precede the coming of the Lord? Before providing a list of events, it would be wise to look at one more verse. Remember that in Jesus' teaching on this subject, He relied on a single prophecy which is clearly worth our attention.

Daniel 9:27 *He* [the beast] *will confirm a covenant with many for one 'seven'* [seven years]. *In the middle of the 'seven'* [at 3½ years] *he will put an end to sacrifice and offering* [in the Jewish temple]. *And at the temple he will set up an abomination that causes desolation, until the end that is decreed is poured out on him.*"

- The man of sin, acting as a man of peace, will make a seven-year covenant with many. This begins the seven-year tribulation. This *covenant* paves the way for the next event.

- This author believes that the seven-year covenant and the rebuilding of the Jewish temple will be part of a protection package that Israel receives with this agreement. However,

87

before this covenant begins it is possible the temple could be built, possibly even years earlier.

The building of the third Jewish temple will be in Jerusalem. There can be no Antichrist or abomination without a Jewish temple. President Trump has made this one step easier by moving the United States embassy and calling Jerusalem the true capital of Israel.

Some churches have tried to spiritualize the rebuilding of the temple by saying that we, the church, are the real temple of God. This is absolutely true. Nonetheless, the third Jewish temple will be built for the old covenant sacrifices. These sacrifices were done away with when Jesus came and established the new covenant. Nevertheless, many Jewish people are still unevangelized and will believe that their sacrifices restore them back to God. They will also believe that the Antichrist [beast] is their long-awaited messiah and will begin to worship him as such.

The Jewish priests will begin the animal and grain sacrifices as in the days of Moses. These sacrifices will go on day and night with great enthusiasm.

Then, after 3½ years the beast will stop the sacrifices and "*set up the abomination that causes desolation*". What is that exactly? Paul relates to us that, "*he sets himself up in God's temple, proclaiming himself to be God*". **2 Thessalonians 2:4**

Not only does he declare himself to be God, but he **demands** to be worshiped by all people. This act of using his newly declared authority as world leader to legally force all people to worship is confirmed in the book of Revelation 13:11-18.

Why will a large majority of people around the world gladly follow and worship the beast? I will show you the reasons in the next few chapters.

This is the breaking of the covenant—the announcement that he is God, followed by his demand to be worshiped. This event represents the beginning of the second half of the 3½ year covenant, which is also called the great tribulation.

We can see more clearly from Paul some of the details of what Jesus taught. Rather than making them easier to digest, Paul paints an even darker picture of the world that we are building for the Antichrist to inhabit and reign over.

Jesus warned us about the great deception that would be present before His return. He said that sin would increase and the love of most [believers] would grow cold. Paul called it an outright rebellion against the God of heaven, and he warned about the man of lawlessness.

Verse five should cause every modern pastor to reconsider what the Christian basics are. **2 Thessalonians 2:5** *"Don't you* remember that when I was with you I used to tell you these things?" When Paul wrote this, he had only been with this new church three or four weeks!

Again, the message and timeline of Christ's return were part of Paul's Christianity 101 class. Now, because of the end time confusion I wrote about in chapter one, we see pastors and seminary professors struggling to answer fundamental questions pertaining to Christ's return.

What is Holding the Antichrist Back?

We know that the timing of the Antichrist's appearance is in the hands of our Sovereign Lord. We know that the Lord Jesus died for a bride, for a church that would glorify Him. The pressure placed on all people by the Antichrist in one moment of time will force wholehearted love for Christ to shine or to be rejected. The Earth will be ripe for the harvest of the righteous and the unrighteous.

First, Population Explosion:

It is estimated that at the time of Christ there was a world population of about 250,000,000 people. Today in 2019, it is estimated that there are 7,500,000,000 people on planet Earth. There are now thirty people for each individual who was on the planet during the time of Christ; that is a thirtyfold increase. The potential harvest for Jesus has grown exponentially.

Second, the Technology Explosion:

For the first time in human history, even with such a great population, mankind has developed a system to link us all together: the internet.

Even though the internet has only been available for consumers and businesses for about twenty-five years, there are almost five billion users of mobile phones at present. Five billion users of a product that was only made available to the general population during the last twenty-five years! The smartphone and the personal computer have linked the world together in astonishing, previously unimaginable ways.

According to **Statista**, a statistical website for researchers, today in 2019, there are 26.6 billion computerized devices connected to the internet. This means that there are over 3.5 devices per each individual on Earth.

We will show later how it is that the most modern technology on the planet will be used to manipulate modern mankind into pledging allegiance to the beast. To ignore the role that technology will play in the end time drama is very dangerous.

Third, Israel:

Prior to Israel's existence in its homeland, the message of Christ's return was spiritualized, symbolized, and effectively thought to be impossible. However, since 1948 the Jewish people have a homeland for the first time in 1,840 years. The Jewish population in Israel now surpasses those murdered in the Holocaust.

From the administration of Jimmy Carter in the late 1970s until the present, president after president of the United States has attempted to broker a peace treaty between Israel and its neighbors, the Palestinians. Of course, in their effort at doing good, they do not realize that they are paving the way for the prophesied man of sin, the beast.

Up until now, all those efforts have failed. However, according to none other than Jesus Christ, **the Jerusalem temple will be rebuilt** and the abomination that causes desolation will set the entire world on a 3½-year path of destruction that will culminate in the literal return of Jesus to the Earth.

Again, what is the power holding back the Antichrist?

2 Thessalonians 2:6-8a *⁶And now you know what is holding him back, so that he may be revealed at the proper time. ⁷ For the secret power of lawlessness is already at work; but the one who now holds it* *back will continue to do so till he is taken out of the way.* *8 And then the lawless one will be revealed…*

God Himself put in place the power that holds back complete lawlessness. Here is an example of how God can hold back things unseen in the book of

Revelation 7:1-3 *After this I saw four angels standing at the four corners of the Earth,* **holding back the four winds of the Earth to prevent any wind from blowing on the land or on the sea or on any tree.** *2 Then I saw another angel coming up from the east, having the seal of the living God. He called out in a loud voice to the four angels who had been given power to harm the land and the sea:* *3* **"Do not harm the land or the sea or the trees until we put a seal on the foreheads of the servants of our God."**

This is a picture of God's angels holding back the destructive forces of judgment. As if our planet was not dark enough already, lawlessness will be released in its fullness. Murder, rape, sexual perversion, human trafficking, addiction, hatred, persecution, witchcraft, genocide, and brazen Satan worship will consume the planet. This all-out lawlessness, of course, emboldens all the inhabitants of the Earth to persecute Jews and Christians to a degree without historical precedent.

Revelation 13:4 *People worshiped the dragon [Satan] because he had given authority to the beast, and they also worshiped the beast and asked, "Who is like the beast? Who can wage war against it?"*

Revelation 13:7-8 *It [the beast] was given power to wage war against God's holy people and to conquer them. And it [the beast] was given authority over every tribe, people, language and nation. 8 All inhabitants of the Earth will worship the beast—all whose names have not been written in the Lamb's book of life, the Lamb who was slain from the creation of the world.*

2 Thessalonians 2:9-12 *The coming of the lawless one will be in accordance with how Satan works. He will use all sorts of displays of power through signs and wonders that serve the lie, 10 and all the ways that wickedness deceives those who are perishing. They perish because they refused to love the truth and so be saved. 11 For this reason God sends them a powerful delusion so that they will believe the lie 12 and so that all will be condemned who have not believed the truth but have delighted in wickedness.*

The beast will have access to all the power of Satan's demonic realm. He will become a master magician and a manipulator at the highest level ever seen. Because they will love wickedness, the people of the Earth will be put under a powerful delusion which will actually be sent by God because they ignored Him, His word, His prophets, and most of all—they rejected His Holy Son Jesus and the sacrifice that Jesus made for them. Now there is nothing left for them but darkness and gloom.

The entertainment media have become bolder and bolder about cursing and blaspheming God as well as presenting all forms of sexual immorality as normal and perfectly acceptable. Now the military, schools, corporations, sports franchises, and almost every vestige of every culture is being pressured into accepting homosexuality and trans sexuality as acceptable, protected, and even promoted as normal.

Luke 17:28-30 *"It was the same in the days of Lot. People were eating and drinking, buying and selling, planting and building. 29 But the day Lot left Sodom, fire and sulfur rained down from heaven and destroyed them all.*

30 *"It will be just like this on the day the Son of Man is revealed.*

As you can see, we are being groomed to accept the lies and blasphemy of the Antichrist as an accepted part of life. In the next chapter, we will investigate the spirit that is driving this.

Revelation 1:12-16

I turned around to see the voice that was speaking to me. And when I turned I saw seven golden lampstands, 13 and among the lampstands was someone like a son of man, dressed in a robe reaching down to his feet and with a golden sash around his chest. 14 The hair on his head was white like wool, as white as snow, and his eyes were like blazing fire. 15 His feet were like bronze glowing in a furnace, and his voice was like the sound of rushing waters.16 In his right hand he held seven stars, and coming out of his mouth was a sharp, double-edged sword. His face was like the sun shining in all its brilliance.

7

THE WORLD IS BEING GROOMED BY THE SPIRIT OF THE ANTICHRIST?

I John 2:18 *"…Even now many antichrists have come…"*

In this chapter, my goal is to show you the importance of knowing the difference between the person of the Antichrist and the spirit of the antichrist. Both the Bible and modern history give us examples that foreshadow the person of the Antichrist. It requires a bit more insight to discern what the Bible calls the spirit of the antichrist. It is this spirit that is connecting the world with one common thought and belief system that will embrace the beast as if he were the true Jewish and world messiah.

The Spirit of Antichrist

The Apostle John gives us the most information about the spirit of antichrist in his first two letters, 1 John and 2 John.

The spirit of antichrist is the spirit working behind the scenes globally in order to groom the people of the world to slowly mold their ideologies to agree more and more with this spirit. Eventually, people will give their full cooperation to follow and then worship this end time, once-in-history person, the beast.

Here are the specific verses where the word "antichrist" is used by John. Notice the **unspectacular** description of the Antichrist and spirit of antichrist.

Nevertheless, it will soon become apparent that on a daily basis we are rubbing shoulders with those who walk, talk, and think in harmony with the spirit of the antichrist.

1 John 2:18 *"Dear children, this is the last hour; and as you have heard that the **antichrist** is coming, even now many **antichrists** have come. This is how we know it is the last hour."*

John declares, **many** antichrists have come.

Here are a few passages that describe how this spirit operates:

I John 2:22 *"Who is the liar? It is **whoever denies that Jesus is the Christ**. Such a person is the **antichrist**—denying the Father and the Son."*

I John 4:3 *"…but **every spirit** that **does not acknowledge Jesus** is not from God. This is the spirit of the **antichrist**, which you have heard is coming and even now is **already** in the world."*

2 John I:7 *"I say this because many deceivers, **who do not acknowledge Jesus Christ as coming in the flesh**, have gone out into the world. **Any such person is the deceiver and the antichrist."***

By reading these easy-to-understand passages with their common-sense meaning, it is easy to observe that the spirit of the antichrist is operating at full throttle in the United States and throughout the world. In Hollywood movies, the name of God and of Jesus Christ is cursed over and over. That is the spirit of antichrist. Science, medicine, education, business, and government have all but wiped the truth about Jesus from the thoughts and hearts of mankind. This is happening all across the United States, the last great bastion of Christianity.

Of course, it goes much further, and in recent times there are those who openly oppose the Jews and Christians. China is trying to crush the Christian church. Many Islamic countries have strict laws against Muslims converting to Christianity. In fact, in many sects of Islam, family members of any new Christian converts are pressured to put the convert to death rather than allow him or her to live as a believer in Christ.

In many European nations church attendance has dropped to between one and three percent. There are strong feelings of anti-Semitism growing across Europe. Jews are living in great fear while living among such hatred and face protests, killings, vandalism, beatings, harassment, and threats on an almost daily basis.

The nation of Israel confronts constant hostility and threats of destruction from their neighbors. In addition, there is a steady onslaught of daily rocket attacks from the Palestinian territory.

Iran continues to threaten to destroy the Jews, and this hatred is continuing to grow around the world. Most of these threats are from Muslim groups. But there are new threats coming from other hate groups as well. Additionally, several members of the United States House of Representatives are now openly anti-

Semitic. And it is actually popular for celebrities to openly oppose doing business with Israel.

Christians, the one group in our country that still opposes homosexuality, transsexuality, and abortion, is labeled as racist!

Much television programming advocates an evolutionary point of view or communicates the idea that someone who believes in the living God is unbalanced. That is the spirit of antichrist.

Global Ideologies

The spirit of antichrist has developed global ideologies. Ideologies are a meaningful set of beliefs used to guide groups of people in the world. Each of the groups listed below have at least twenty-five percent of the world's population.

False Religions and Humanism

The first area of influence by this spirit are false religions that deny that Jesus, God's Son, came to Earth, died for the sin of mankind, and has been raised to life and ascended to the right hand of God.

This includes Hinduism, Buddhism, Islam, Mormonism, Masonry, and Jehovah's Witnesses. False religion extends to all who justify themselves by their own good works.

This includes everyone who labors under the banner of secular humanism, atheism, science, and medicine as well as modern educational systems. Additionally, it provides the framework for philosophy, psychology, and social welfare run by governments. **Clearly, there are many godly individuals who labor within these systems.** Notwithstanding their commitments to perform their duties with excellence unto the Lord, it will become increasingly difficult for them to prosper in these environments because of increasing resentment and hatred.

Oppressive Governments

The second major antichrist ideology has to do with various governmental forms that shut Christ out of the public thinking. These systems not only despise Christ, but they impose their views on others. I believe this is especially true with communism, fascism, and socialism. These forms of government rule over China, Russia, Cuba, North Korea, Vietnam, Myanmar, and many others. Of course, the United States has begun walking down the same road during the last forty to sixty years.

Capitalism

The third major antichrist ideology is capitalism. This provides a unique challenge for people like us in the USA who were raised under this powerful ideology. To us, it's all we've ever known. In fact, other systems seem inferior and perhaps even ungodly. Yet how many small wars and how many millions of people have been slaughtered and enslaved over land, oil, diamonds, and other resources that were needed to expand capitalism?

Islam

The fourth major antichrist ideology is Islam. This faith has grown quickly to include one-fourth of the world's population. Distinct from Buddhism or Hinduism, Islam has a global vision to take over the world. Islam is radically and universally antichrist in nature. Every place where Islam gains a foothold and establishes itself as a significant percentage of the population, it communicates a strong aversion to both Jews and Christians.

All of these ideologies are attractive to their proponents. There are thousands and even millions of well-meaning and noble people in every one of these four groups. However, these major ideologies are playing a huge role in ushering in the person of the Antichrist.

Many of these individuals may love religion and doing good deeds. Unfortunately, they operate as pawns under the power of this global spirit. They serve in government, medicine, science, academics, or as volunteers, but they have one thing in common: they have rejected Jesus, the Christ of the Bible.

Foreshadowing the Person of the Antichrist

The person of the Antichrist has been referred to by many different names so far. He is seen more vividly through historic character types. They are actual men who have lived in Bible times and more recent history.

These men have all risen to near-superpower status with a demonic and ruthless treatment of the Jewish and or Christians under their dominion.

As you consider these historic leaders, nearly all of them were revered by their followers as gods. Yet, in comparison, all these men will be dwarfed by the beast of Revelation.

A Short List

- **The Pharaoh of Egypt** enslaved 600,000 Jewish men and as many women. Pharaoh ruthlessly oppressed the Jewish people as slaves for many decades. At one point the Jews were multiplying so fast that Pharaoh commanded all the newborn boys to be thrown into the Nile river to be eaten by crocodiles.

- **Nebuchadnezzar** decimated the city of Jerusalem after a long siege ending in 586 BC. His army destroyed the first Jewish temple and killed almost every Jew in the region except for a few thousand who were brought to Babylon as slaves. This king was treated as a god by his people and built a ninety-foot statue of gold in his honor. All people, free and slave, were commanded to worship the statue or be throw into a fiery furnace.

- **The Roman Caesars** were worshiped as gods. They oppressed the Jews throughout Israel during their reign. In 64 AD Nero made Christianity illegal throughout the Roman Empire and found various ways to kill Christians, causing many to renounce their faith rather than be tortured.

- **The Roman general Titus, under** Caesar's command, destroyed Jerusalem and the Jewish temple in 70 AD, killing over one million Jews in the process.

- **Mohammad's** new religion of Islam at the beginning of 610 AD sought to kill all Jews. Islam has grown to the second largest religion in the world with over 1.5 billion followers. Muslim persecution of Jews and Christians continues in every country or region where Islam gains a stronghold.

- **Adolph Hitler** mesmerized his followers with his demonic and passion-filled rage. His speeches filled his Nazi followers with murder that killed over six million Jewish civilians in Europe and 1.5 million more in Ukraine during his Holocaust of World War II. This was only seventy-five years ago, as of this writing. The startling thing about Hitler's persecution was his relentless desire to kill every Jew: women, children, the old, and helpless were all killed. In only the rarest cases could the wealthy or those of high position escape with bribes.

In Ukraine it is estimated there are over 2,000 mass graves where over 1,500,000 Jews were killed and buried. The Jewish populace from almost every city, town, and village in Ukraine were rounded up by special Nazi death squads, machine gunned, and buried by the local townspeople. One grave was excavated where 34,000 bodies were buried.

Here are some examples of the drastic change in the Jewish population from the time of Hitler's rise to power in prewar 1933 compared to postwar 1950. The four nations where the Jewish population was most devastated are seen below.

Poland: before 3,000,000, after 45,000

Germany: before 565,000, after 37,000

Czechoslovakia: before 357,000, after 17,000

Austria: before 250,000, after 18,000

Europe's total population before was 9,500,000 and after was 3,500,000

These leaders like Hitler were each a **foreshadowing** of the person of Antichrist. He will be revealed finally as the beast of

Revelation 13. Each of these reprehensible historical characters were operating in the spirit of the antichrist.

In the final days, hatred against Israel and the church will swell like a great tsunami over the Earth.

Revelation 12:17 *"Then the dragon Satan was enraged at the woman [Israel] and went off to wage war against the rest of her offspring [Christians]—those who keep God's commands and hold fast their testimony about Jesus."*

While this battle intensifies, God is raising up an army of young, old, rich, poor, those high and low who will hold on to Jesus' word and the testimony declaring His victorious return to the Earth. But first we must face up to serious trouble coming on the Earth before we will ever prepare for it.

Revelation 7:9-12

9 After this I looked, and there before me was a great multitude that no one could count, from every nation, tribe, people and language, standing before the throne and before the Lamb. They were wearing white robes and were holding palm branches in their hands. 10 And they cried out in a loud voice:

"Salvation belongs to our God, who sits on the throne,
and to the Lamb."

11 All the angels were standing around the throne and around the elders and the four living creatures. They fell down on their faces before the throne and worshiped God, 12 saying:

"Amen!
Praise and glory and wisdom and thanks and honor
and power and strength be to our God for ever and ever.
Amen!"

8

THE BEAST OF REVELATION 13

Let's take ten minutes to read eighteen amazing verses from the book of Revelation. It is jam packed with details and word pictures to describe this man of sin that appears at the end of the age to deceive the world into believing that he is the true messiah. After we read this chapter, we will read it again and I will make some comments to put this text into today's terminology.

Revelation 13

The dragon stood on the shore of the sea. And I saw a beast coming out of the sea. It had ten horns and seven heads, with ten crowns on its horns, and on each head a blasphemous name. [2] *The beast I saw resembled a leopard but had feet like those of a bear and a mouth like that of a lion. The dragon gave the beast his power and his throne and great authority.* [3] *One of the heads of the beast seemed to have had a fatal wound, but the fatal wound had been healed. The whole world* was filled with wonder and followed the beast. 4 People worshiped the dragon because he had given authority to the beast, and they also worshiped the beast and asked, "Who is like the beast? Who can wage war against it?"

5 The beast was given a mouth to utter proud words and blasphemies and to exercise its authority for forty-two months. 6 It opened its mouth to blaspheme God, and to slander his name and his dwelling place and those who live in heaven. 7 It was given power to wage war against God's holy people and to conquer them. And it was given authority over every tribe, people, language and nation. 8 All inhabitants of the Earth will worship the beast—all whose names have not been written in the Lamb's book of life, the Lamb who was slain from the creation of the world.

9 Whoever has ears, let them hear.

10 "If anyone is to go into captivity,
    into captivity they will go.
If anyone is to be killed with the sword,
with the sword they will be killed."
This calls for patient endurance and faithfulness on the part of God's people.

The beast out of the Earth

¹¹ Then I saw a second beast, coming out of the Earth. It had two horns like a lamb, but it spoke like a dragon. ¹² It exercised all the authority of the first beast on its behalf, and made the Earth and its inhabitants worship the first beast, whose fatal wound had been healed. ¹³ And it performed great signs, even causing fire to come down from heaven to the Earth in full view of the people. ¹⁴ Because of the signs it was given power to perform on behalf of the first beast, it deceived the inhabitants of the Earth. It ordered them to set up an image in honor of the beast who was wounded by the sword and yet lived. ¹⁵ The second beast was given power to give breath to the image of the first beast, so that the image could speak and cause all who refused to worship the image to be killed. ¹⁶ It also forced all people, great and small, rich and poor, free and slave, to receive a mark on their right hands or on their foreheads, ¹⁷ so that they could not buy or sell unless they had the mark, which is the name of the beast or the number of its name.

¹⁸ This calls for wisdom. Let the person who has insight calculate the number of the beast, for it is the number of a man. That number is 666.

Revelation 13

The dragon stood on the shore of the sea. And I saw a beast coming out of the sea. It had ten horns and seven heads, with ten crowns on its *horns, and on each head a blasphemous name. ² The beast I saw resembled a leopard but had feet like those of a bear and a mouth like that of a lion. The dragon gave the beast his power and his throne and great authority.*

[The dragon is Satan, and he authorizes a man, the beast, to rule on his behalf. The ten horns he has represent ten kings that align with the beast. The further description of the leopard, bear and the lion likely hint at three of these kingdoms. There is much disagreement on who these nations are. The important thing we should know is that the beast builds a strong coalition of nations that will make a seven-year treaty with Israel. This treaty will ensure that the Jewish temple is rebuilt while Israel is protected by this covenant.

If the power dynamics in the world are not altered significantly between now and the time when these events occur, the United States will be one of the key players, if not the key player in this treaty. It is Israel's only true ally and protector. Every president since Jimmy Carter in the mid-1970s has been working on this treaty with Israel and the Palestinians. Billions of dollars have been invested and immense effort made to forge a treaty on behalf of Israel. As I write, President Trump is working on the "deal of the century", as he calls it. Somehow, the beast will be backed by nations with substantial military and financial power.]

³ One of the heads of the beast seemed to have had a fatal wound, but the fatal wound had been healed.

[This fact about the beast is rarely mentioned, but here it is: **He is killed or assassinated and then raised from the dead.** This resurrection from the dead will surely play a large part in deceiving the nations into believing that he is the true messiah. This matter with the beast being raised from the dead is also mentioned in verses 12 and 14.

Three times Revelation shows us that the Antichrist will be struck dead and raised again from the dead! Certainly, he will deceive the world by mirroring the resurrection of the true Christ, Jesus. This will happen midway into the seven-year treaty. This explains why all the world will worship him.]

³bThe whole world was filled with wonder and followed the beast.
⁴ People worshiped the dragon because he had given authority to the beast, and they also worshiped the beast and asked, "Who is like the beast? Who can wage war against it?"

[So we see that after the beast is raised from the dead, he goes from international peacemaker to global deity. The whole world will be captivated by the beast. The beast is now set to consolidate his power. This will happen in Jerusalem at the rebuilt Jewish temple.]

5 The beast was given a mouth to utter proud words and blasphemies and to exercise its authority for forty-two months. 6 It opened its mouth to blaspheme God, and to slander his name and his dwelling place and those who live in heaven. 7 It was given power to wage war against God's holy people and to conquer them. And it was given authority over every tribe, people, language and nation. 8 All inhabitants of the Earth will worship the beast—all whose names have not been written in the Lamb's book of life, the Lamb who was slain from the creation of the world.

[It seems likely that the mouth the beast is given is total backing of the global media. Just a few years ago the media seemed to be fair and impartial, but what is normal in communist countries and banana republics has now come to America as well. The media will be a powerful tool in the hands of the beast. As the gloriously celebrated beast makes his way to Jerusalem, he will be celebrated as the global messiah at every stop. On every talk show and at every press conference, the world media will be fawning over this great man of peace who was just **raised from the dead**. They hang on his every word and follow him everywhere, celebrating. Allowing the drama to build to a fever pitch, he is yet to confirm or deny his deity. The media makes the declaration for him— surely, he is the Jewish messiah and is the Lord of the Earth.

The other Messiah, "Jesus Christ of the Bible is a myth. The Bible is a fairy tale," they say rhetorically. "Do you want a 2,000-year-old Messiah," they ask, or one who is "here today that you can see, hear and touch?"]

⁹ Whoever has ears, let them hear. ¹⁰ "If anyone is to go into captivity, into captivity they will go. If anyone is to be killed with the sword, with the sword they will be killed." This calls for patient endurance and faithfulness on the part of God's people.

[In this passage believers are being warned that prison and death awaits those who oppose the beast. There will be so many true believers hauled to prison that concentration camps will need to be rebuilt. We are to expect persecution. The Bible warned about these days, and at this very moment they will have arrived.]

The beast out of the Earth

¹¹ Then I saw a second beast, coming out of the Earth. It had two horns like a lamb, but it spoke like a dragon.

[This is a second beast, and you can think of it as the beast's public relations firm. His job is to enhance the mystique surrounding the beast and to carry out the logistics needed to prepare Jerusalem and the Jewish temple for the most exciting event the world will ever experience.]

¹² It exercised all the authority of the first beast on its behalf, and made the Earth and its inhabitants worship the first beast, whose fatal wound had been healed. ¹³ And it performed great signs, even causing fire to

*come down from heaven to the Earth in full view of the people. ¹⁴ Because of the signs it was given power to perform on behalf of the first beast, it deceived the inhabitants of the Earth. It ordered them to set up an image in honor of the beast **who was wounded by the sword and yet lived.***

[To get a picture of what is about to happen you can read Daniel chapter 3. In mid-500 BC the king of Babylon, Nebuchadnezzar, has a massive statue constructed that is ninety feet tall. This statue represents the king's greatness. Then the king commands his leaders and employees from all over the empire to appear before the statue. He commands them to fall down in worship before the statue when music is played. In the event that anyone dares to defy this order, the tyrant announces that person will be thrown into the fiery furnace.]

¹⁵ The second beast was given power to give breath to the image of the first beast, so that the image could speak and cause all who refused to worship the image to be killed.

[This is the "abomination that causes desolation" that Daniel, Jesus and Paul warn us about. **This is the key sign that triggers the great tribulation, and it notifies us that Jesus will be returning in only about 3½ years.**]

¹⁶ It also forced all people, great and small, rich and poor, free and slave, to receive a mark on their right hands or on their foreheads, ¹⁷ so

117

that they could not buy or sell unless they had the mark, which is the name of the beast or the number of its name.

[All of the prelude has finished and one of the greatest days in human history has arrived—the unveiling of the beast as the Jewish messiah and leader of the whole Earth. Up to this time, he has been thought of exclusively as the man of peace. Daniel 3 is reenacted on a global scale. Because of the beast's great deception, his media support, his death and resurrection, and the promotional acumen of the second beast, the nations choose to worship him. They want to be part of his vision for the Earth. "How do we unite in the cause?" they are asking. This author estimates that eighty percent of the global population will gladly take his "mark" within the first few days. What will happen to those who resist? The following verse answers this unequivocally.]

15b the image could speak and cause all who refused to worship the image to be killed. 16 It also forced all people, great and small, rich and poor, free and slave, to receive a mark on their right hands or on their foreheads, 17 so that they could not buy or sell unless they had the mark, which is the name of the beast or the number of its name.

[In 1990, merely thirty years ago, the internet was invented. Americans and those around the world have shifted from cash to cashless societies. Our shopping, bill paying, investments, and even our paychecks arrive via the internet. Even those who pay cash still mostly pay with a bank card. All of our finances, except those hidden in our mattresses, are under the watchful eye of the internet. For generations people have been trying to figure out what the mark of the beast is.

Now it is obvious, the mark of the beast will be a biometric system to give his followers access to the internet.]

Revelation 13:16-17 *It also forced all people, great and small, rich and poor, free and slave, to receive a mark on their right hands or on their foreheads,*

*so that **they could not buy or sell unless they had the mark, which is the name of the beast or the number of its name.***

[Because of the beast's mighty coalition, he will not only gain control of the nations and the media but will also exercise dominion of the internet. This is of supreme importance. Those who take his mark have full access to the internet, and their banking privileges are intact. They can buy and sell freely.

Contemplate the following scenario. Imagine waking up in the morning with no access to the internet. You have been red-flagged. You must now have the beast's permission to get into your internet accounts. How do you get permission? Simply by pledging allegiance to the beast on your smartphone or computer screen.

In regard to the beast, you will need only to submit your right palm print and an eye scan to accept the beast's leadership and Lordship for your life, and your access will be restored. Your banking is restored you can buy and sell again.

The mark of the beast is now solved!

It's simple—biometrics. Biometrics is literally the unique measurement of a man or woman. Biometrics are being experimented with and perfected on a daily basis. There are hundreds of corporations investing billions of dollars in almost every nation to make biometric security a universal possibility.

Biometrics are used for giving access or denying access in all aspects of life: border crossings, airport security, banking, surveillance and of course, access to some computer systems. The beast will simply gain power to deny access to anyone who will not give him their allegiance.

The pressure on resisters will be immense. They are pressured by the media, the culture, their friends and neighbors. "Get with the program, take the mark," they say. Next, the beast shuts all resisters out of the internet, they can't buy and sell. Everything they have worked for is inaccessible: their banking, homes, cars, retirement, groceries, gas and health care. They are locked out of the financial system and their homes and cars certainly will be repossessed. **Multiple millions of Christians will count the cost and quickly surrender, taking the mark of the beast.** For true believers, they will have counted the cost far in advance. They will be prepared for this event. They will leave their homes and possessions to become fugitives.]

Urgent Warning to Christian Leaders

It will be an act of supreme negligence for believers to observe the peace treaty, the rebuilding of the temple, the animal sacrifices restored and not be prepared by this point in time. For this reason, it is incumbent on pastors and leaders to become knowledgeable about the end time chronology. The current season of relative calm allows us to adjust our theology and practice so that our congregations can enter into the coming season of difficulty with sobriety.

Athletic teams begin their seasons with grueling practice sessions in the sweltering heat of July and August because coaches know that toughness must be built into their charges on the front end. There must be sufficient physical, mental and relational strength to endure through the severe challenges ahead.

In the same way, Christian leaders, like coaches, must do everything they can to prepare their people for the coming days.

Certainly, the reward that awaits us far exceeds an earthly trophy.]

[18] *This calls for wisdom. Let the person who has insight calculate the number of the beast, for it is the number of a man. That number is 666.*

Revelation 14:6-7

Then I saw another angel flying in midair, and he had the eternal gospel to proclaim to those who live on the earth—to every nation, tribe, language and people. 7 He said in a loud voice, "Fear God and give him glory, because the hour of his judgment has come. Worship him who made the heavens, the earth, the sea and the springs of water."

9

OVERCOMING THE BEAST

The Call to Surrender All

Mark 8:35 *For whoever wants to save their life will lose it, but whoever loses their life for me and for the gospel will save it. 36 What good is it for someone to gain the whole world, yet forfeit their soul?*

The beast's plans are made known as we read and study the book of Revelation. He will deceive a great majority of humanity, acquire great power on a worldwide scale and then force everyone into an "either-or" dilemma. Most people will opt to take the mark of the beast in order to participate fully in society as they have done up to this point. Conversely, those who refuse to take this mark will be locked out of the economic system and will be regarded as criminals both by the government and society at large. Modern church life in the West has not prepared us for the following harsh reality: This will be a season of intense persecution, martyrdom and great struggle. Perhaps there will be cities of refuge and lands of Goshen throughout the world; we must hope that this will be the case. Nevertheless, all believers will be confronted with the stark choice of submitting to the world's demonic system or remaining faithful to Jesus while accepting the sacrifices it will demand.

In Matthew 24 Jesus teaches on the days leading up to His return, and there is clear call to prayer. The same is true in Mark 13 where Jesus gives the same teaching and the same exhortation: watch and pray. Similarly, this pattern continues in Luke 21, 2 Thessalonians and 2 Peter.

Having a lifestyle of prayer will lead us into a way of life that loves generosity as we identify with the sufferings of Jesus and the church around the world. This will give us a keener discernment of the times and prepare us to suffer gladly. Perhaps all will not suffer equally, but we must all prepare to endure hardship.

Take a moment to read this parable. This is a continuation of the end time teaching in Matthew 24.

The Wise and Foolish Virgins

Matthew 25:1-13 *"At that time the kingdom of heaven will be like ten virgins who took their lamps and went out to meet the bridegroom. ² Five of them were foolish and five were wise. ³ The foolish ones took their lamps but did not take any oil with them. ⁴ The wise ones, however, took oil in jars along with their lamps. ⁵ The bridegroom was a long time in coming, and they all became drowsy and fell asleep.*

⁶ "At midnight the cry rang out: 'Here's the bridegroom! Come out to meet him!'

⁷ "Then all the virgins woke up and trimmed their lamps. ⁸ The foolish ones said to the wise, 'Give us some of your oil; our lamps are going out.'

⁹ "'No,' they replied, 'there may not be enough for both us and you. Instead, go to those who sell oil and buy some for yourselves.'

¹⁰ "But while they were on their way to buy the oil, the bridegroom arrived. The virgins who were ready went in with him to the wedding banquet. And the door was shut.

¹¹ "Later the others also came. 'Lord, Lord,' they said, 'open the door for us!'

¹² "But he replied, 'Truly I tell you, I don't know you.'

13 "*Therefore keep watch, because you do not know the day or the hour.*"

I believe that the wise virgins had a genuine Spirit-filled life of prayer as well as an understanding that the Bridegroom, Jesus, would be coming late and at a time of deep darkness. The foolish virgins were unprepared. They expected to be taken out before the darkness. They had neither deep prayer nor sufficient understanding. For this reason, they were locked out of the wedding celebration.

Luke includes a strong exhortation from Jesus to pray during this season of difficulty.

The Trap and the Bait

Luke 21:34-36 "*Be careful, or your hearts will be weighed down with carousing, drunkenness and the anxieties of life, and **that day will close on you suddenly like a trap**. 35 For **it will come on all those who live on the face of the whole Earth**. 36 Be always on the watch, and pray that you may be able to **escape all** that is about to happen, and that you may be able to stand before the Son of Man.*"

Since this trap will come suddenly on the whole Earth, Jesus was giving His devoted followers a way to escape. Do not misunderstand! **The escape is *not* a secret rapture.** We know from Revelation 13 that the **trap includes heavy deception that features a death and resurrection**. In Paul's writing he describes a deception so strong that he terms it a delusion.

A few synonyms for the word delusion include misunderstanding, illusion and hallucination. This delusion will be powerful and convincing.

In addition to the delusion, there is a powerful economic element to this ambush. For a trap to be effective there needs to be bait so compelling that people, even believers, will be willing to risk their very souls to obtain it.

What is the bait? Stop and think about this again. Could it be your money, lifestyle or property? When everything that you have worked for and all of your future is on the line, can you walk away from it? Or will you be like the rich young ruler? He kept his riches but was full of regret. This is not some vain, hypothetical scenario but rather the very real dilemma that is soon to confront multitudes of believers.

Luke 18:22-23 *When Jesus heard this, he said to him, "You still lack one thing. Sell everything you have and give to the poor, and you will have treasure in heaven. Then come, follow me."* [23] *When he heard this, he became very sad, because he was very wealthy.*

Give Away Our Belongings!

How can we get free from the desire to have more of the world's pleasures and possessions? How do we reduce our dependence upon the material aspect of our lives?

We must start increasing our giving of finances and we must grow in prayer. Don't beat yourself up because of a lack of prayer in your life. Instead, make learning about prayer, praying and finding a healthy prayer meeting a priority.

Next, we must prepare our hearts to go without. Jesus models this perfectly after His teaching on His return in Luke 21. Let's look at the first and last verses of Luke 21.

Luke 21:2-4 *He also saw a poor widow put in two very small copper coins. ³ "Truly I tell you," he said, "this poor widow has put in more than all the others. ⁴ All these people gave their gifts out of their wealth; but she* **out of her poverty put in all she had to live on.**"

The next thirty-one verses Jesus devotes to teaching on the end times. Then we read this unusual fact about Jesus.

Luke 21:37 *Each day Jesus was teaching at the temple, and each evening* **he went out to spend the night on the hill called the Mount of Olives,**

Jesus could have easily received an offering to bless the widow. And He could have stayed in a luxury room. But Jesus always walking the walk shows us that being a poor widow or sleeping outside at night does not affect who you are in the kingdom.

What is the trap that Jesus just spoke of in Luke 21:34? It is both the mark of the beast and the deceptive culture of materialism that has been developed by the spirit of antichrist.

I believe this is exactly why the Holy Spirit led Luke to begin chapter 21 with the story of the offerings at the temple and to close the chapter with the observation about Jesus spending each night sleeping outside.

The widow gave everything she had and trusted God to meet her needs. Jesus slept outside demonstrating that His kingdom was not of this world.

Regardless of whether He was praying or sleeping, Jesus told the truth when he said:

Luke 9:58 *Jesus replied, "Foxes have dens and birds have nests, but the Son of Man has no place to lay his head".*

In this passage, like many others, Jesus is stating that poverty is permissible. Yes, He was voluntarily living in poverty. Why? Perhaps it was so that He would not be tempted to abandon His mission due to the comfort of wealth. If sleeping outside for a few nights was acceptable for Jesus, then it should be sufficient for us.

Maybe Jesus is also teaching us that following Him may cost us even the roof over our heads, along with many other extras to which we feel entitled.

Of course, Jesus chose a lifestyle that very few others in our culture would embrace unless we were forced to do so. The mark of the beast will press us into embracing a lifestyle of generosity, and perhaps even poverty.

What will happen after we have been forced to surrender all of our earthly goods? We can enter into a blessedness that only comes through true poverty.

Matthew 5:3 *Blessed are the **poor in spirit**, for theirs is the kingdom of heaven.*

Luke 6:20 *Looking at his disciples, he said: "**Blessed are** you who **are poor**, for yours is **the** kingdom of God".*

131

It is amazing to observe how many people come to Christ when they hit rock bottom. Tragic, challenging life experiences such as divorce, bankruptcy, job loss, major illness or the death of a family member force us to confront the insignificance of a strictly material existence. Although some get bitter, many are suddenly open to the reality of a God who is watching over them and cares for them. The gospel suddenly means something; maybe this is your experience.

This is what poverty of spirit looks like. Suddenly, when you find yourself in a mess, the kingdom of heaven becomes real and it opens its door to you. Next, you meet the God of love and His supernatural provision.

So the mark of the beast really will be a blessing in disguise. It will cause millions around the Earth to be in this blessed state. We must recall that Jesus declared, "blessed are the poor". Let's read the whole passage.

Luke 6:20-26 *Looking at his disciples, he said: "Blessed are you who are poor, for yours is the kingdom of God. 21 Blessed are you who hunger now, for you will be satisfied. Blessed are you who weep now, for you will laugh. 22 Blessed are you when people hate you, when they exclude you and insult you and reject your name as evil, because of the*

Son of Man. **23** *"Rejoice in that day and leap for joy, because great is your reward in heaven. For that is how their ancestors treated the prophets.* **24** *"But woe to you who are rich, for you have already received your comfort.* **25** *Woe to you who are well fed now, for you will go hungry. Woe to you who laugh now, for you will mourn and weep.* **26** *Woe to you when everyone speaks well of you, for that is how their ancestors treated the false prophets.*

From one moment to the next, every Christian on the planet will not be able to buy or sell. All of us will be paupers unless the Lord provides lands of refuge where the persecution is not so intense, and we happen to live there or can flee there. The beast will have bankrupted every true believer.

Poverty, Prayer and Power

So what will we do in this state of blessed poverty? We will gather together and pray. Finally, our minds will be free from the grip of media, money and time. We will have real fellowship and will sing just like Paul and Silas did in the Philippian prison. We will live with the kingdom of heaven at our disposal.

The miracles of the Bible—healing, protection and miraculous provision—will be available to His faithful ones. Also we will face hardship, severe persecution and sometimes death. We will live in forests, deserts, abandoned buildings and farmhouses.

Please do not hold on to the idea that you will get to keep your house and car, as this is unlikely.

I believe that in the world of the beast, his followers will become beastlike. Furthermore, in the world of the beast, only the beastlike will rule. We will have Christ. We will have the power of the Spirit and access to miracles.

Yet at the same time mobs will most likely ask you to leave your house and possessions. If you do not comply, I believe that force will be used. I apologize for the previous statement—I really do not enjoy writing this. Nonetheless, it is true.

As I mentioned earlier, for any trap to be effective there must be bait that attracts the victim to risk being ensnared. What is the bait for which you are willing to surrender your eternal future?

Is it simply unimaginable that you will have to forfeit your property? If so, ask yourself the following question: Does your total lifestyle really belong to Jesus? Decide right now to surrender your life, comfort and possessions to Jesus Christ, whose blessings are eternal.

As a brother or sister in the Lord, make the right choice.

Revelation 22:16-21

"I, Jesus, have sent my angel to give you this testimony for the churches. I am the Root and the Offspring of David, and the bright Morning Star."

17 The Spirit and the bride say, "Come!" And let the one who hears say, "Come!" Let the one who is thirsty come; and let the one who wishes take the free gift of the water of life.

18 I warn everyone who hears the words of the prophecy of this scroll: If anyone adds anything to them, God will add to that person the plagues described in this scroll. 19 And if anyone takes words away from this scroll of prophecy, God will take away from that person any share in the tree of life and in the Holy City, which are described in this scroll.

20 He who testifies to these things says, "Yes, I am coming soon."

Amen. Come, Lord Jesus.

Summary of events to look for in days ahead:

1. The church is confused about the end times and Christ's return.

2. Israel is restored as a nation, but it depends upon relationships with powerful nations for its protection so that it can rebuild its temple.

3. Technological advances permit global surveillance over the vast majority of the Earth's population.

4. Satan uses technology to spread and deepen the message of the spirit of antichrist. This prepares the world for the appearance of the beast.

5. Prophecies regarding the "days of Noah" and "days of Lot" come to full measure as godlessness and aberrant sexual behavior become commonplace. Lawlessness will run rampant in many places across the Earth. Simultaneously, there is a great falling away from God.

6. The beast's appearance precedes Christ's return. (2 Thessalonians 2, Matthew 24, Mark 13)

7. The beast will confirm a seven-year treaty with Israel and other nations. This makes way for the rebuilding of the Jewish temple and animal sacrifices. (Daniel 9:27)

8. The church is still confused, asleep and in unbelief. These key signs will occur completely unnoticed by vast numbers of nominal Christians. Possibly, even some dedicated Christians will be unaware due to negligence among church leaders.

9. The beast's seven-year reign will consist of two parts. It begins with a covenant between Israel and many other nations. For the first 3½ years the beast enjoys unprecedented favor. He charms the media, public and leaders of the nations. The beast is the media's golden boy and is esteemed by nearly the entire world; some speak of him possibly being the true Jewish messiah and even the king of the whole Earth. Astutely, he merely nods approvingly at such lofty conjecture because he is aware that his big moment is yet to arrive.

10. At some point during the 3½ year period the beast will suffer a fatal wound, perhaps by assassination. It will devastate his followers.

11. Then, in spectacular fashion, he will be raised from the dead—just like Jesus.

12. He will invite the world's leaders and the public to meet him in Jerusalem for a special announcement. He will promise to unveil the plan that he was given by his "Father in heaven" while he was "asleep". This announcement will take place on a global livestream for the entire world to witness.

13. The abomination of desolation begins as the beast announces publicly at the Jewish temple that he is God and demands to be worshiped. He legislates for personal devotion as the one true messiah. Loyalty will be demonstrated by taking his mark via some internet-connected device.

14. Hundreds of millions from around the world will take the mark of the beast on the very first day, and this will include multiple millions of Christians who have been deceived. Within weeks, the global masses also take the mark.

15. Once people take this mark they are eternally condemned by God. There is no turning back. Their consciences are seared, and they worship and serve the beast. Like the beast, they will have unbounded hatred for Jews and Christians.

16. Those who refuse to take his mark are automatically locked out of all technology, then they will be imprisoned

or slain. Within several weeks, five to six billion will take the mark. Those who resist are regarded as enemies of global peace. Friends, neighbors, relatives and workmates receive substantial monetary rewards for turning in these subversives to the government. Since those who take the mark will have no conscience, they will gladly cooperate because they believe that this is service to God and a form of patriotism. There will be much martyrdom. All will not be killed, but all believers will have to weigh up the cost of choosing Christ rather than taking the mark.

17. The beast's revealing will usher in genuine New Testament Christian life. There will be authentic community and prayer. In fact, it may result in global revival among the resisting Christians.

18. For the first time since the first-century church, Christians will enjoy true unity on a large scale. They will be grouped together in a variety of settings such as campgrounds, farmhouses, forests and fields. They will live in makeshift quarters and abandoned buildings; everything will be shared. Being locked out of the internet will produce true fellowship. It is likely that the leaders will not be talented speakers or administrators but rather will be like the apostles of old. They will heal the sick, multiply food, expose false brothers and provide genuine shepherding.

19. There will be miraculous answers to prayer along with global judgments which are released in response to global worship and intercession.

20. The Lord will return at the darkest moment. He will be seen by every living person. While the faithful rejoice and are being taken up in the air, the world will mourn.

21. Jesus will take revenge on His enemies and promote His saints into eternal wealth and prosperity. Most importantly, they will reign with Him forever!

Revelation 12:11

They triumphed over him
by the blood of the Lamb
and by the word of their testimony;
they did not love their lives so much
as to shrink from death.

FINAL THOUGHTS

I have served as a leader in the church for over twenty years with a focus on building prayer and a deeper Christian life. I have served as a pastor of prayer in a local church, a regional leader and a missionary.

The Christian leaders I have interacted with have been genuine, earnest and bright with a solid foundation in the Bible. They sincerely love Jesus and are well educated. Many hold masters or doctorate degrees from well-known seminaries. They are zealous for church growth and evangelism.

Yet there is an alarming indifference when it comes to the subject of the return of Christ.

Why? The message of the return of the Lord concerns subjects rarely mentioned in our modern church: persecution, suffering, martyrdom and great loss. Most of all, it speaks of a dramatic change in our vision and goals for the future.

Perhaps the Laodicean church in Revelation 3 represents most closely the current church in the United States. Our material wealth, national security, beautiful facilities, talented pastors and excellent programs have lulled us to sleep.

Listen to the language Jesus uses to wake this church from its sleep.

Revelation 3:17 *You say, 'I am rich; I have acquired wealth and do not need a thing.' But you do not realize that you are wretched, pitiful, poor, blind and naked.*

How can a nation as great as ours really understand weakness?

Paul understood that the gospel rested on God's power and not its own. The stark truth is that God is after the heart of mankind, not its power, wealth or influence. Church leaders will change one at a time by God's grace. Only then will they affect the congregations.

2 Corinthians 12:9 *But he said to me, "My grace is sufficient for you, for my power is made perfect in weakness." Therefore, I will boast all the more gladly about my weaknesses, so that Christ's power may rest on me.*

Teaching on the return of the Lord is vital.

2 Timothy 4:2-4 *Preach the word; be prepared in season and out of season; correct, rebuke and encourage—with great patience and careful instruction. 3 For the time will come when people will not put up with sound doctrine. Instead, to suit their own desires, they will gather around them a great number of teachers to say what their itching ears want to hear. 4 They will turn their ears away from the truth and turn aside to myths.*

God will prune His Vine; the only question is: Will today's leaders cooperate with Him in obedience?

I urge you to become a heroic voice for the Lord as His return approaches.